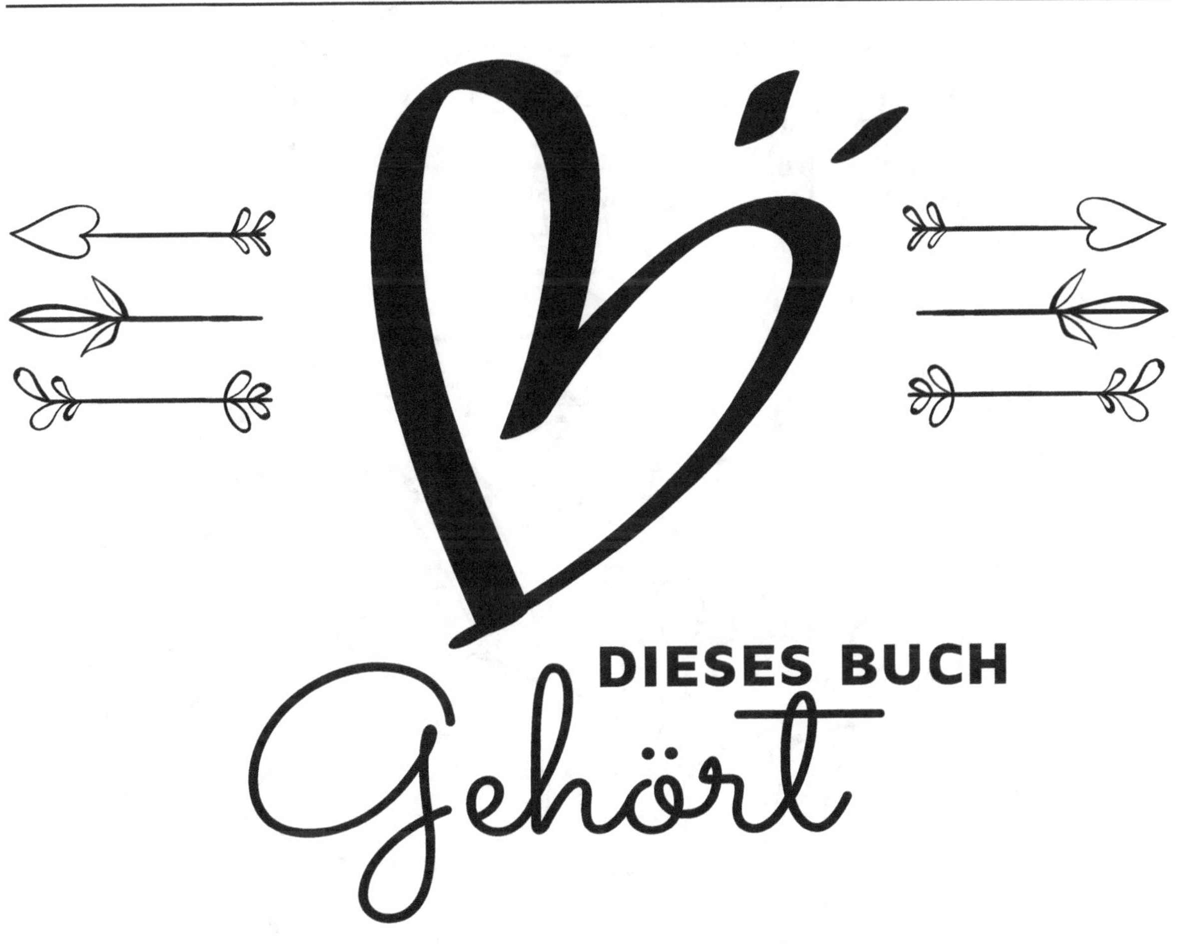

DIESES BUCH
Gehört

MONSTER TRUCK MALBUCH

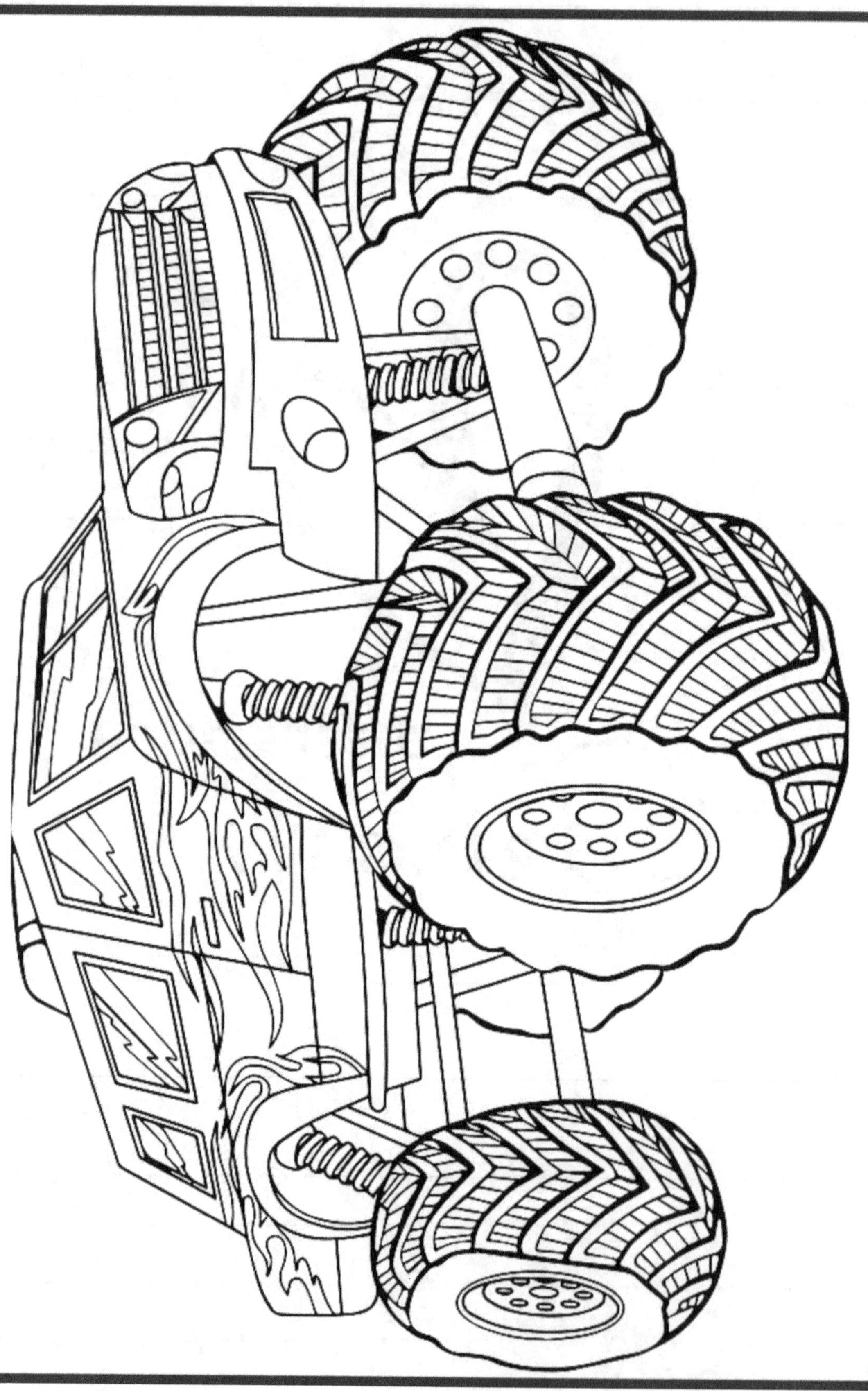

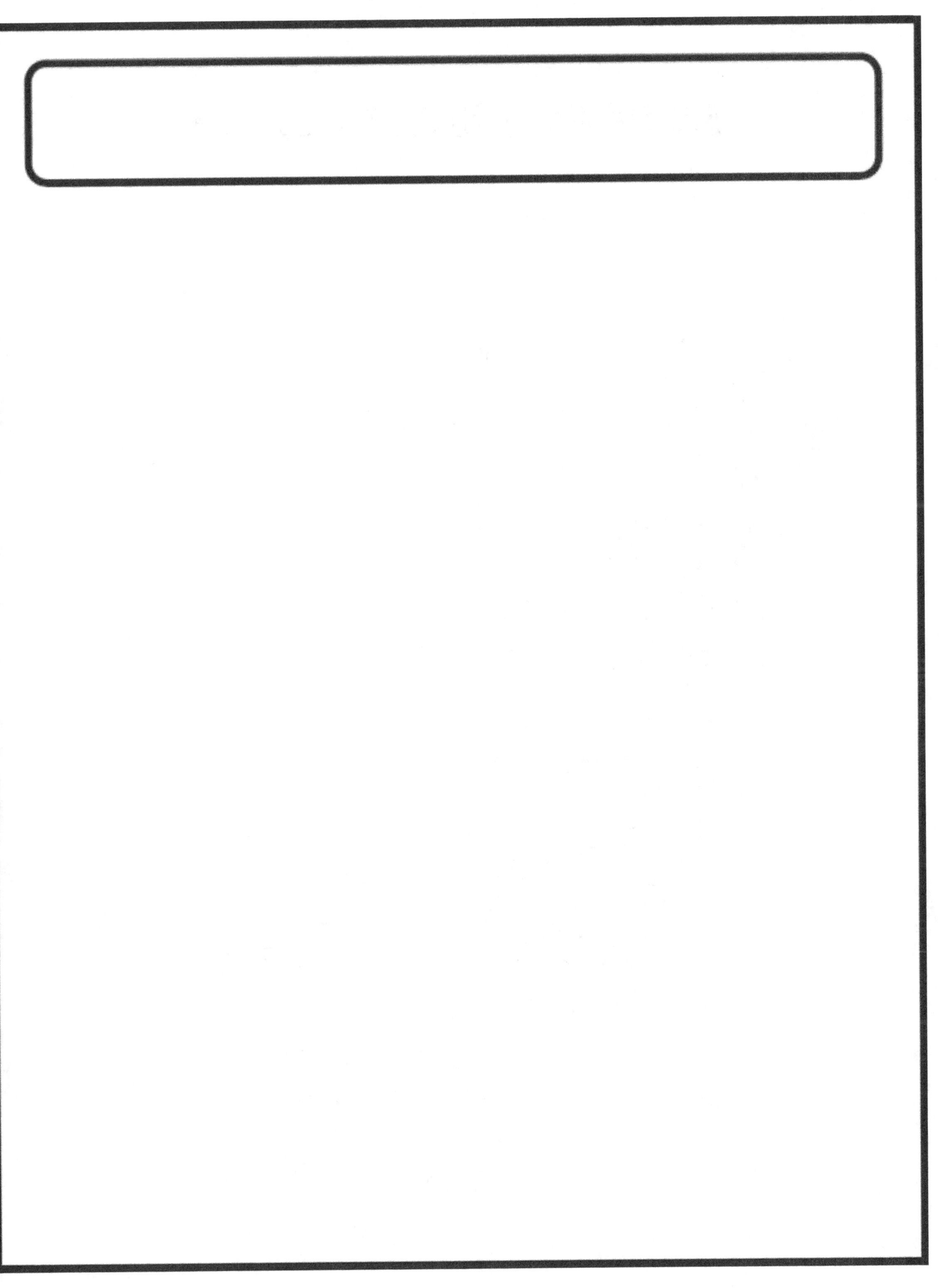

MONSTER TRUCK MALBUCH

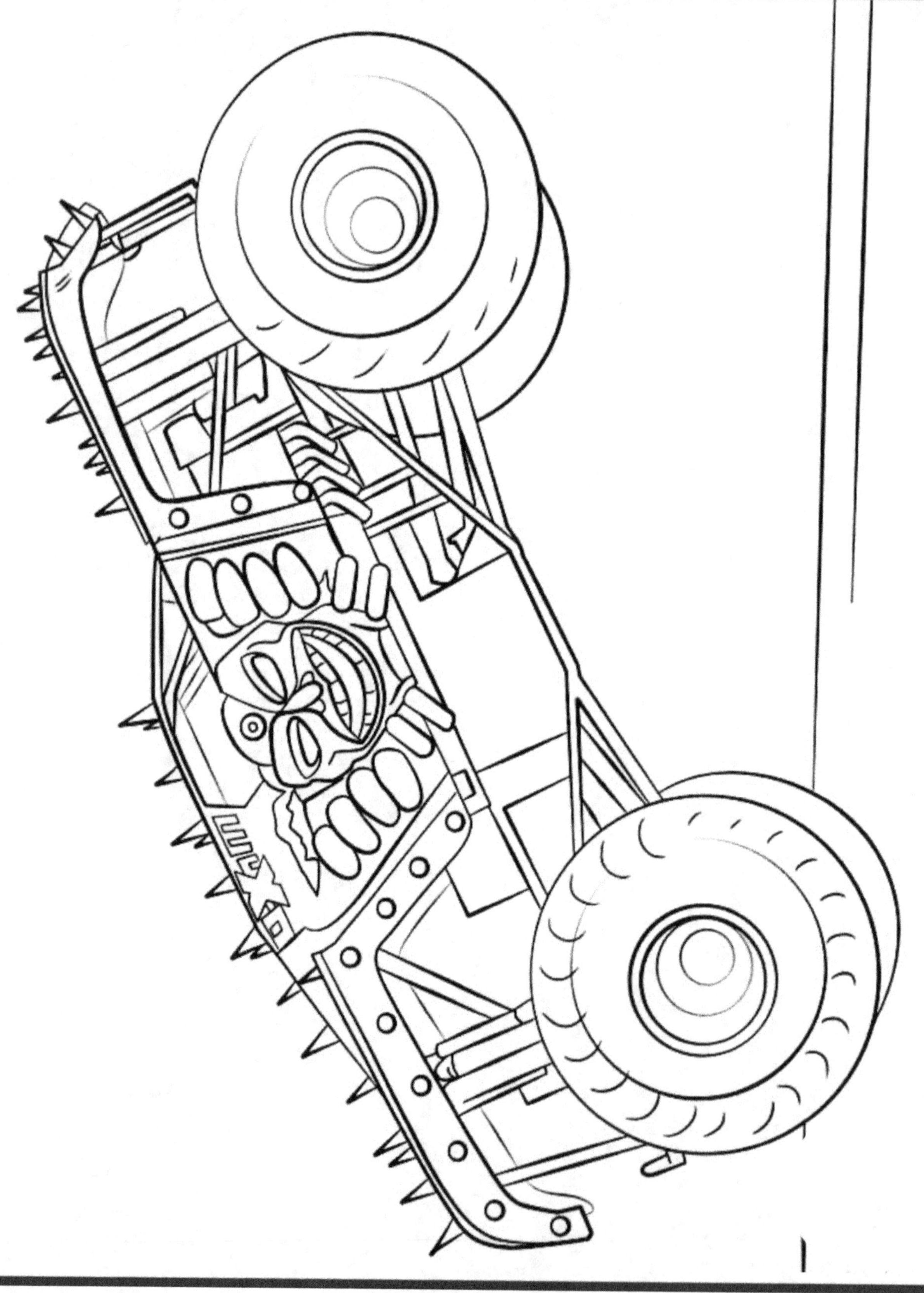

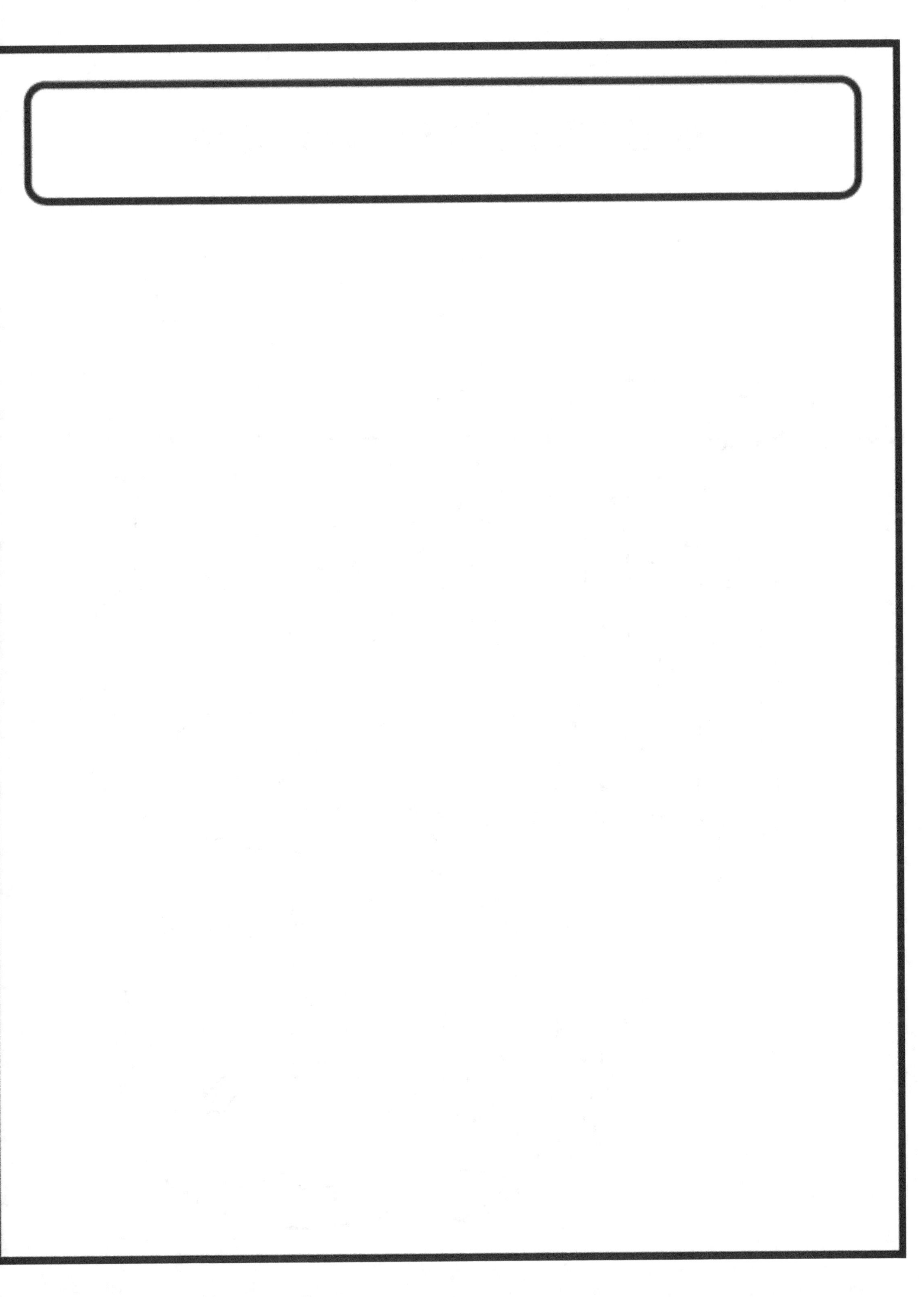

MONSTER TRUCK MALBUCH

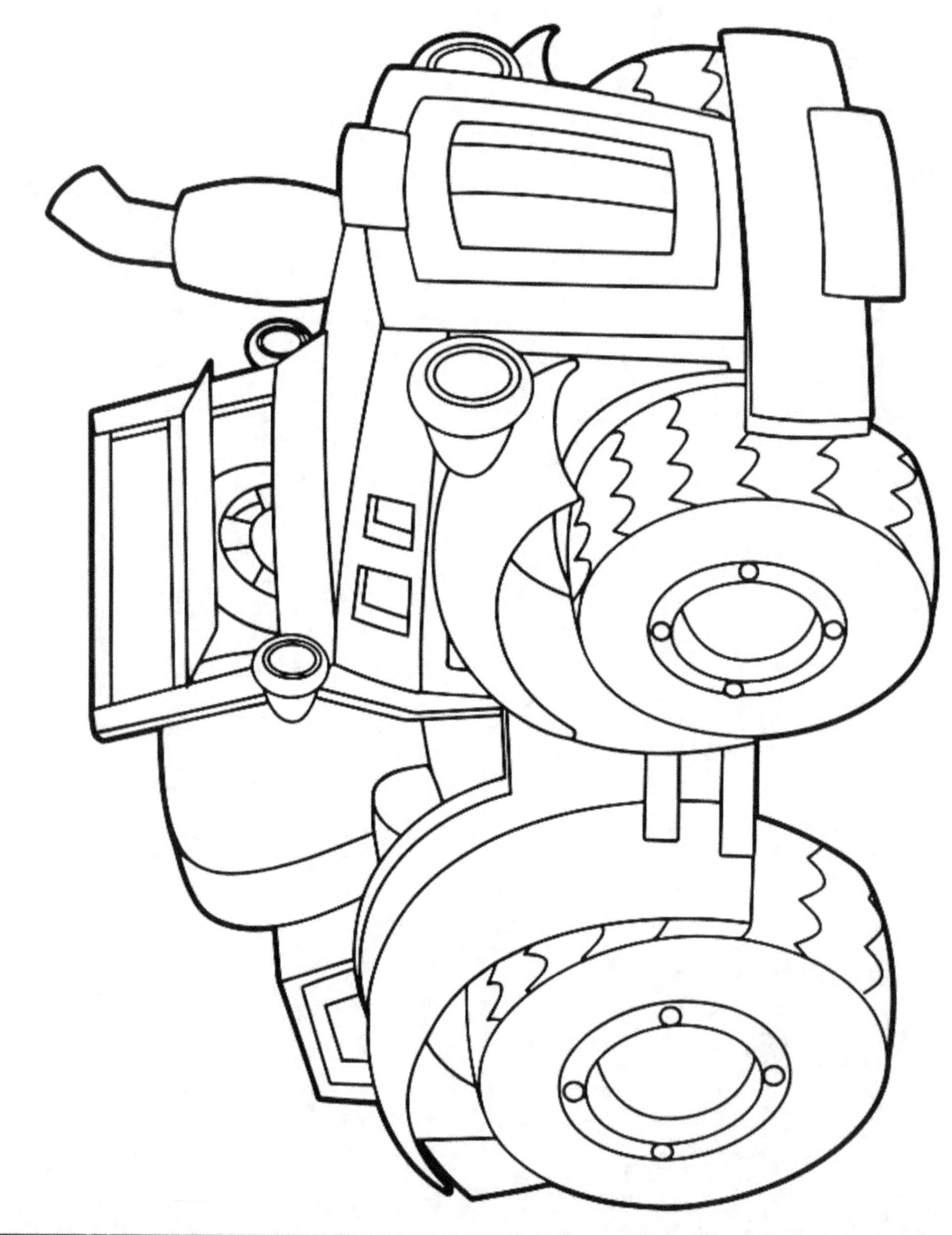

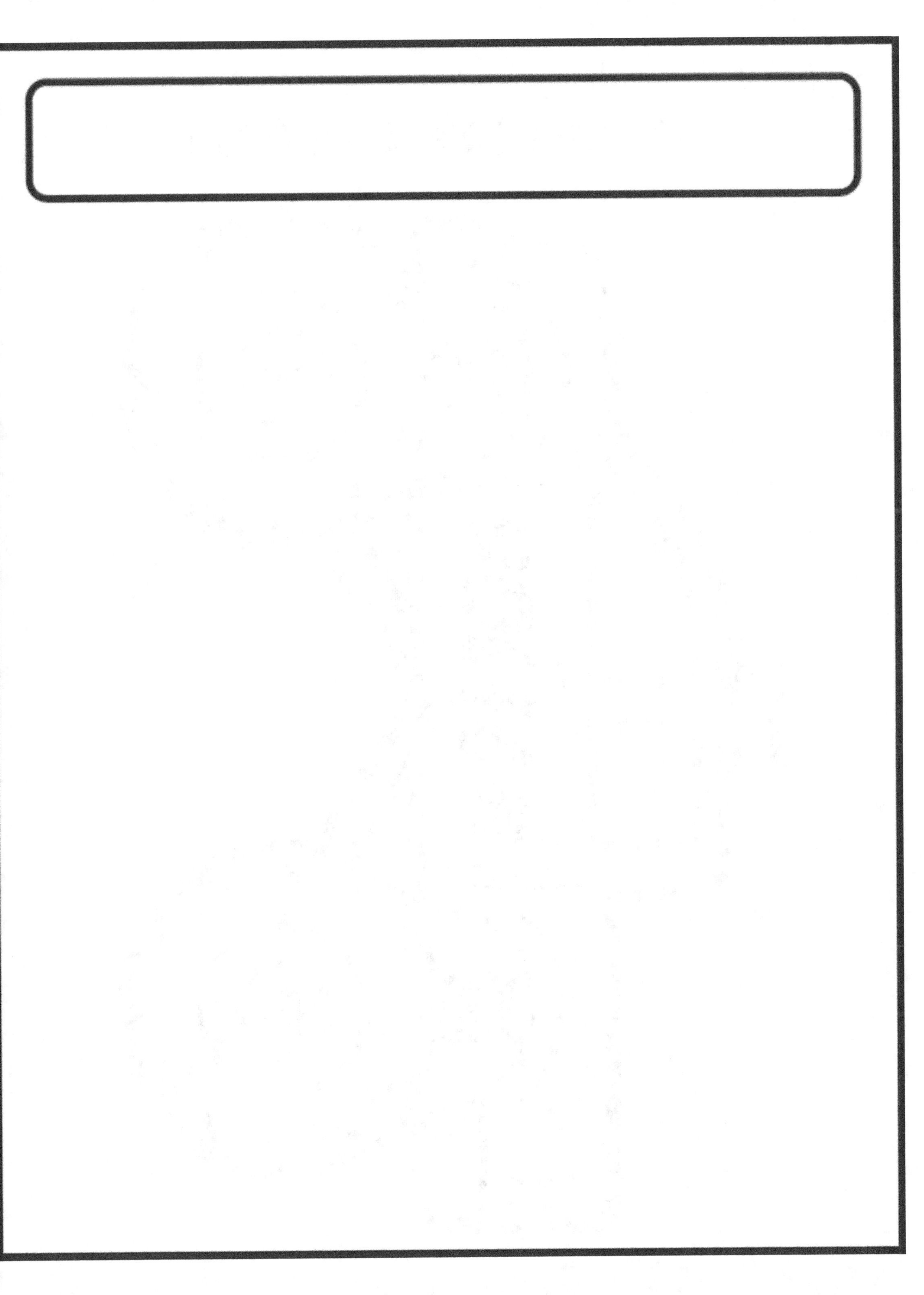

MONSTER TRUCK MALBUCH

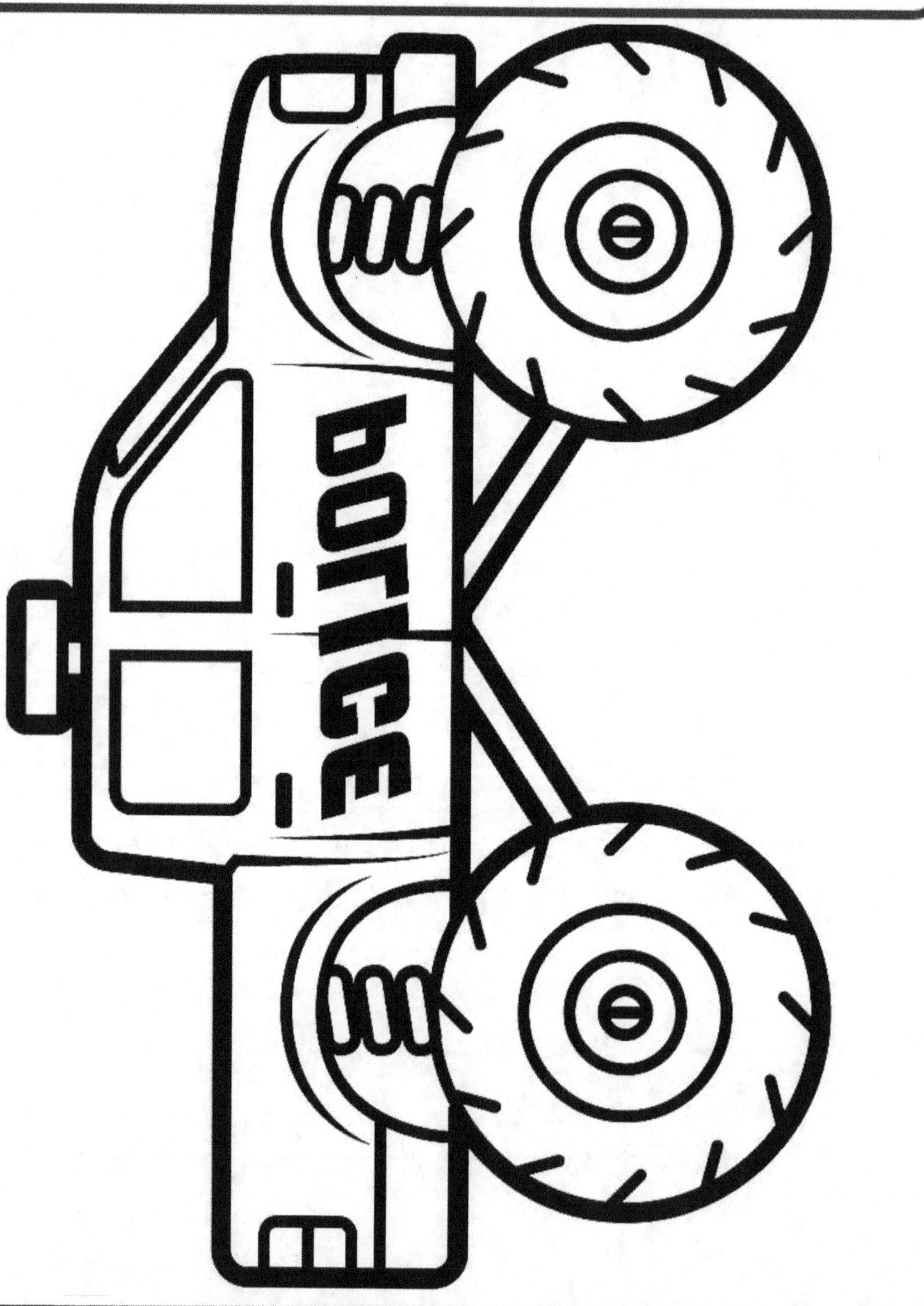

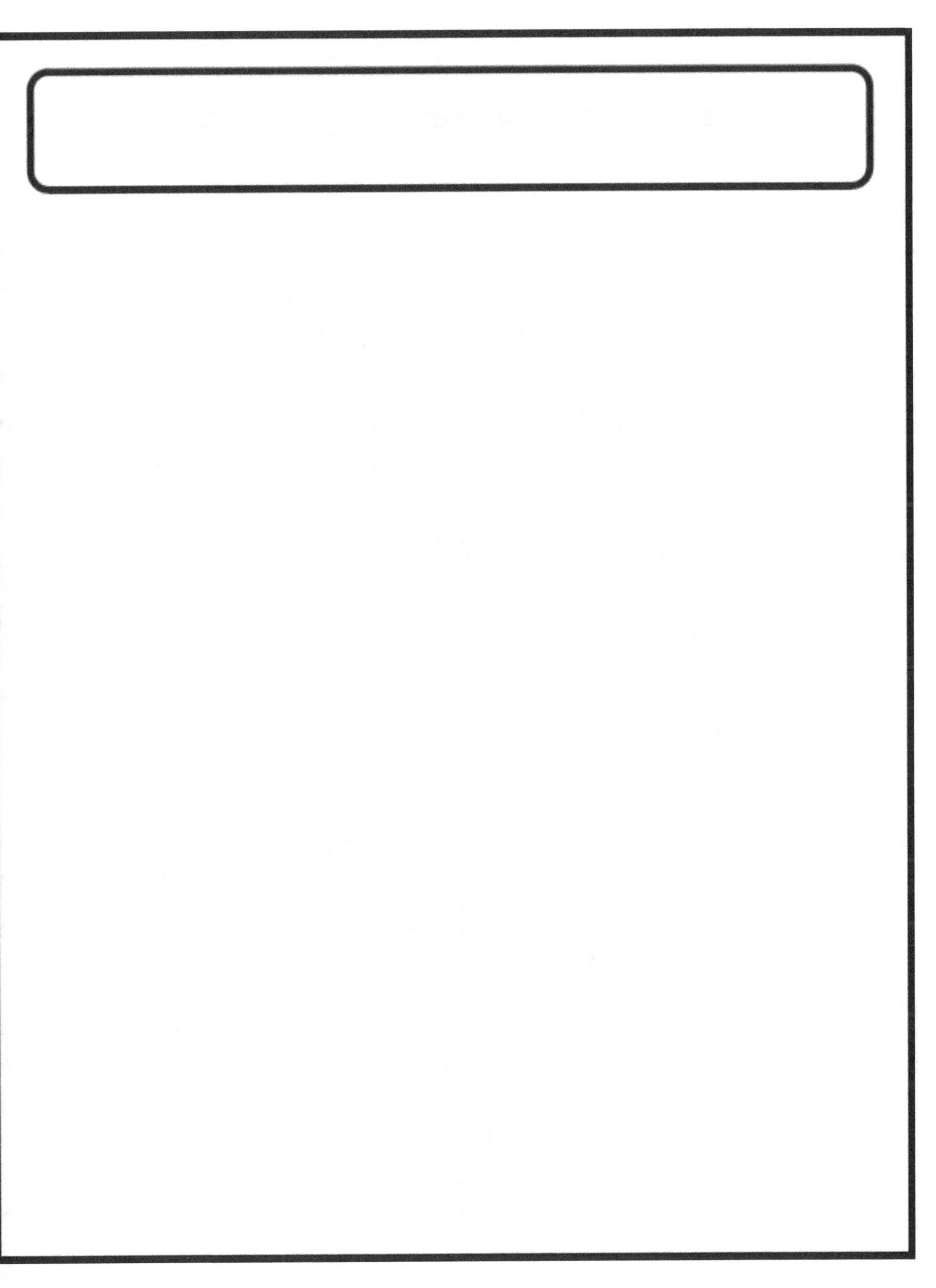

MONSTER TRUCK MALBUCH

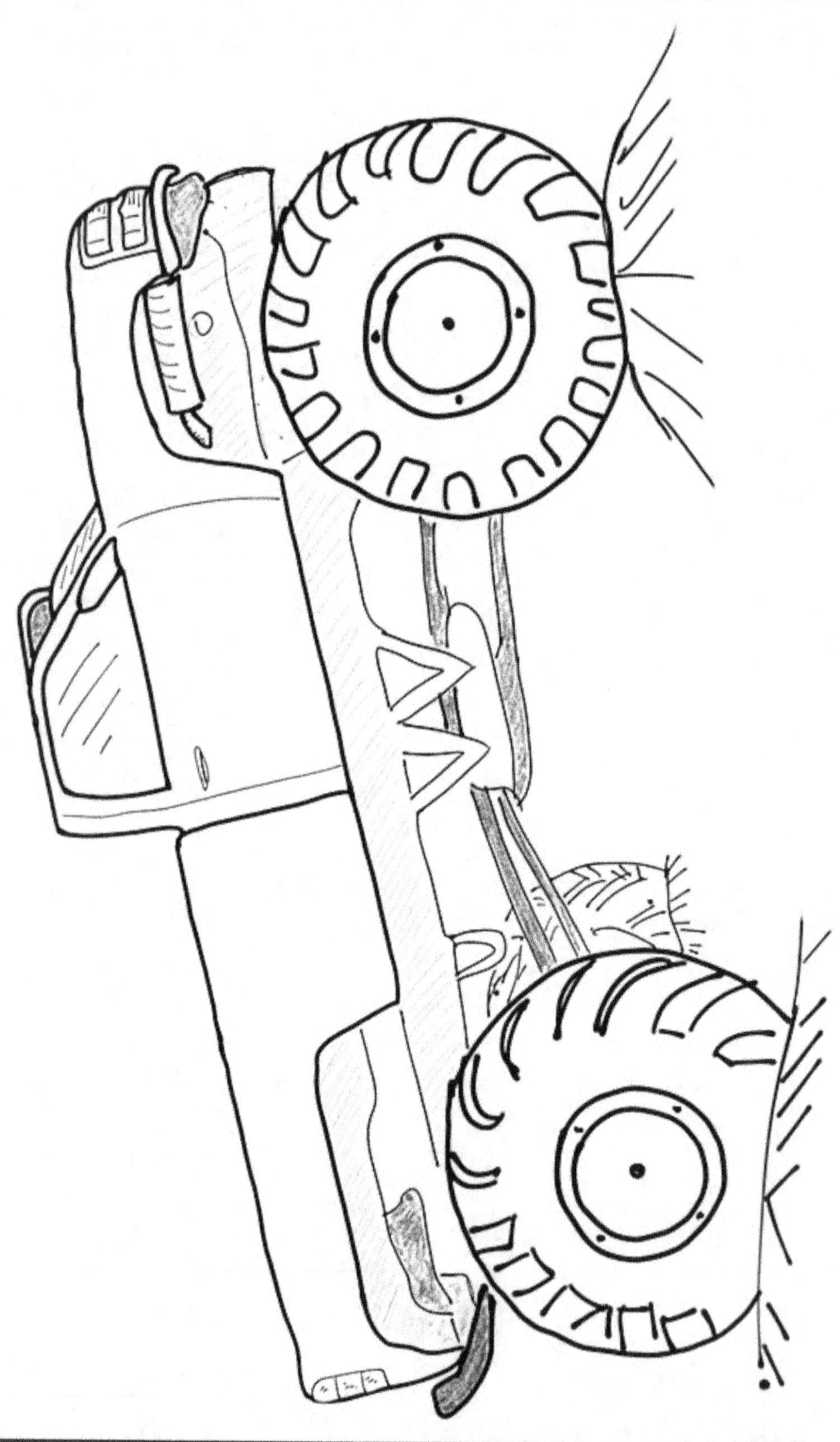

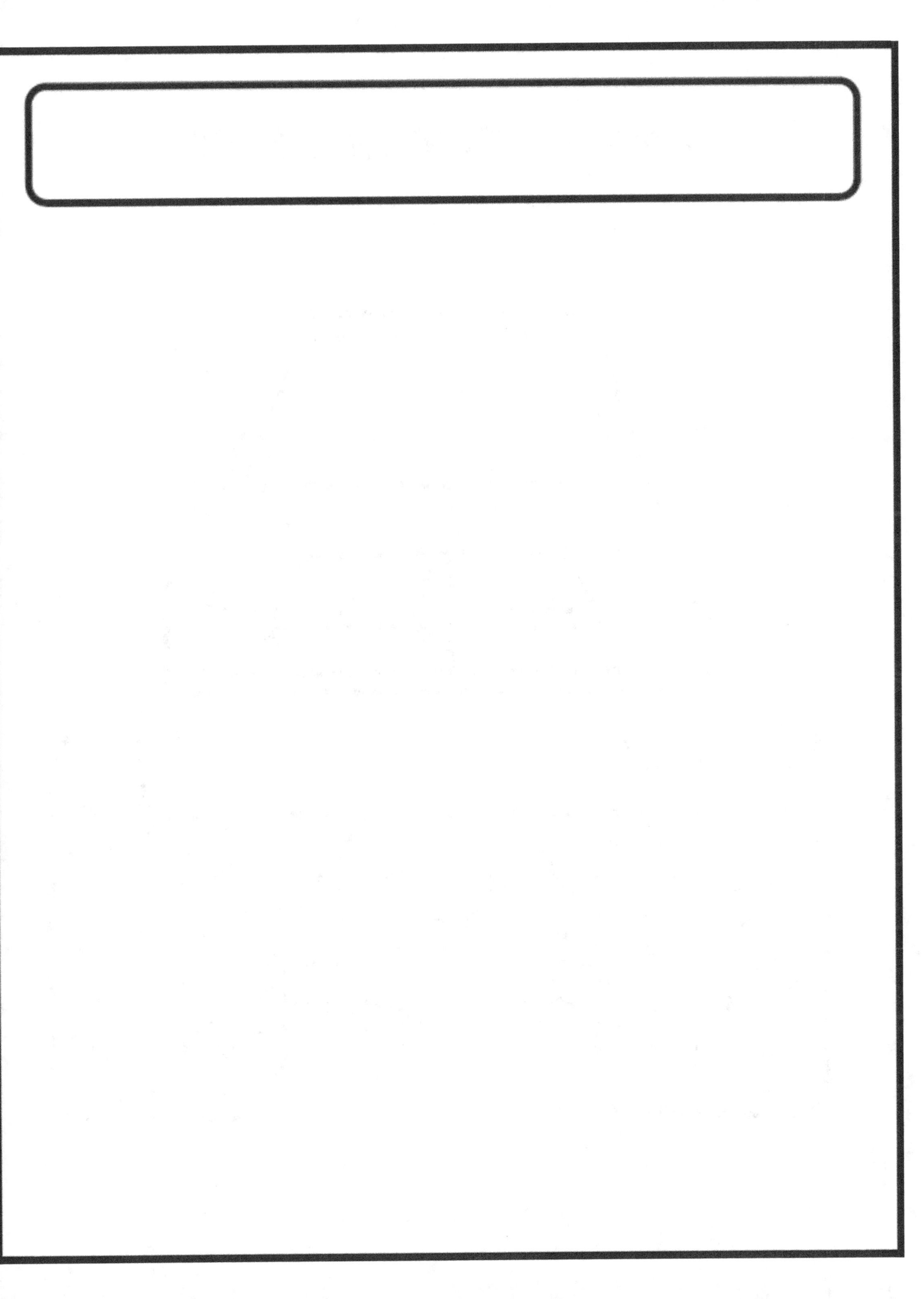

MONSTER TRUCK MALBUCH

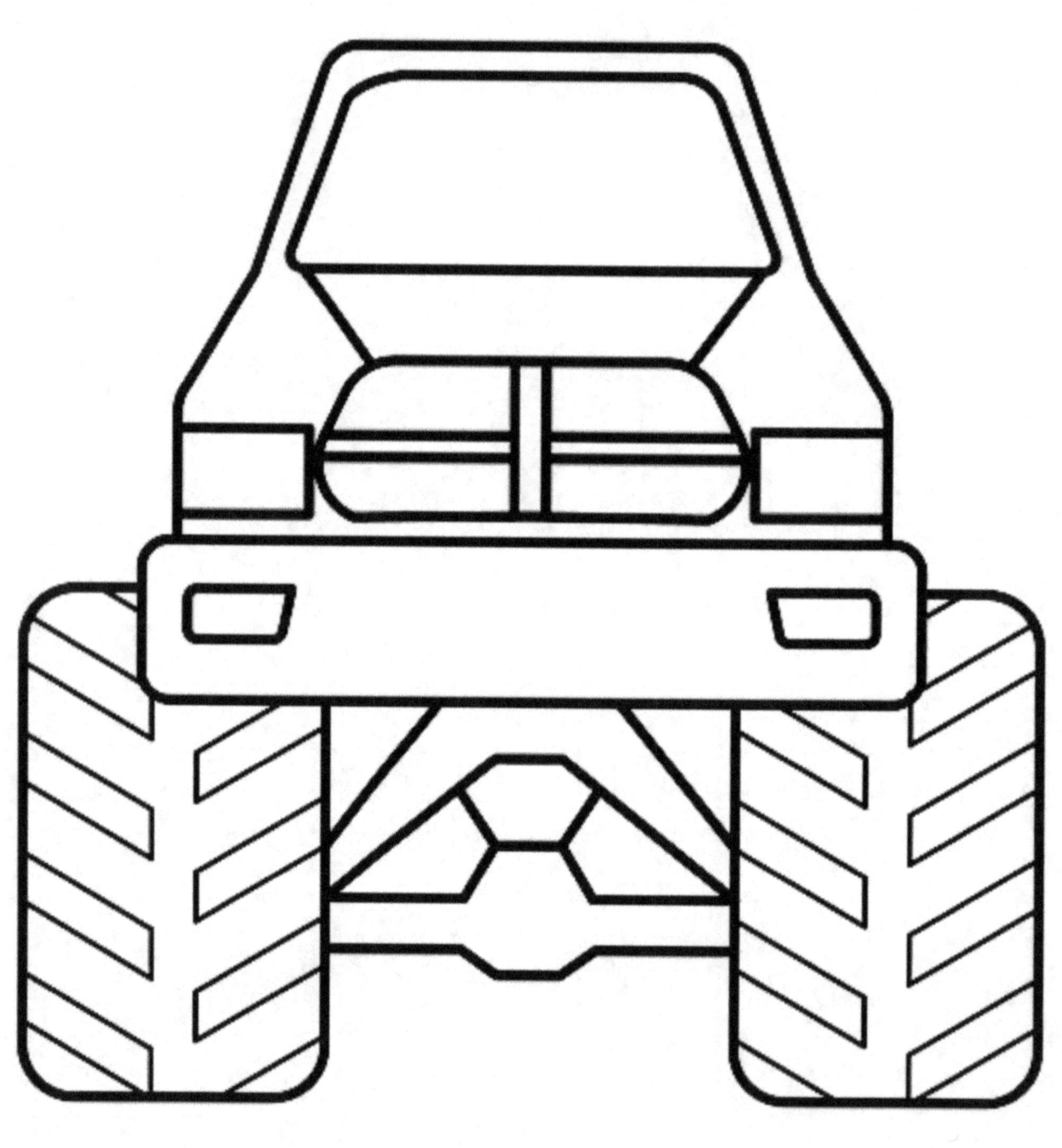

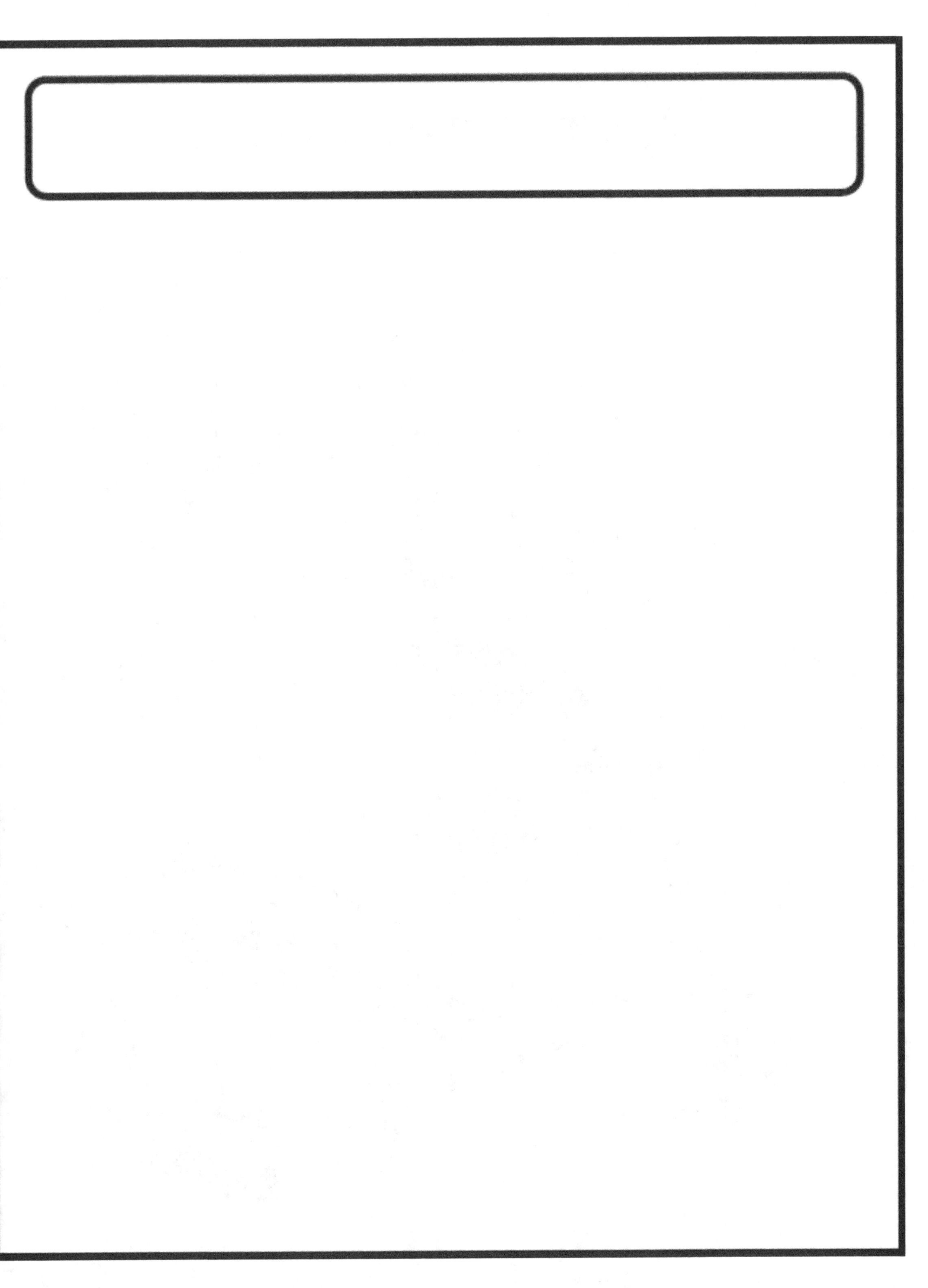

MONSTER TRUCK MALBUCH

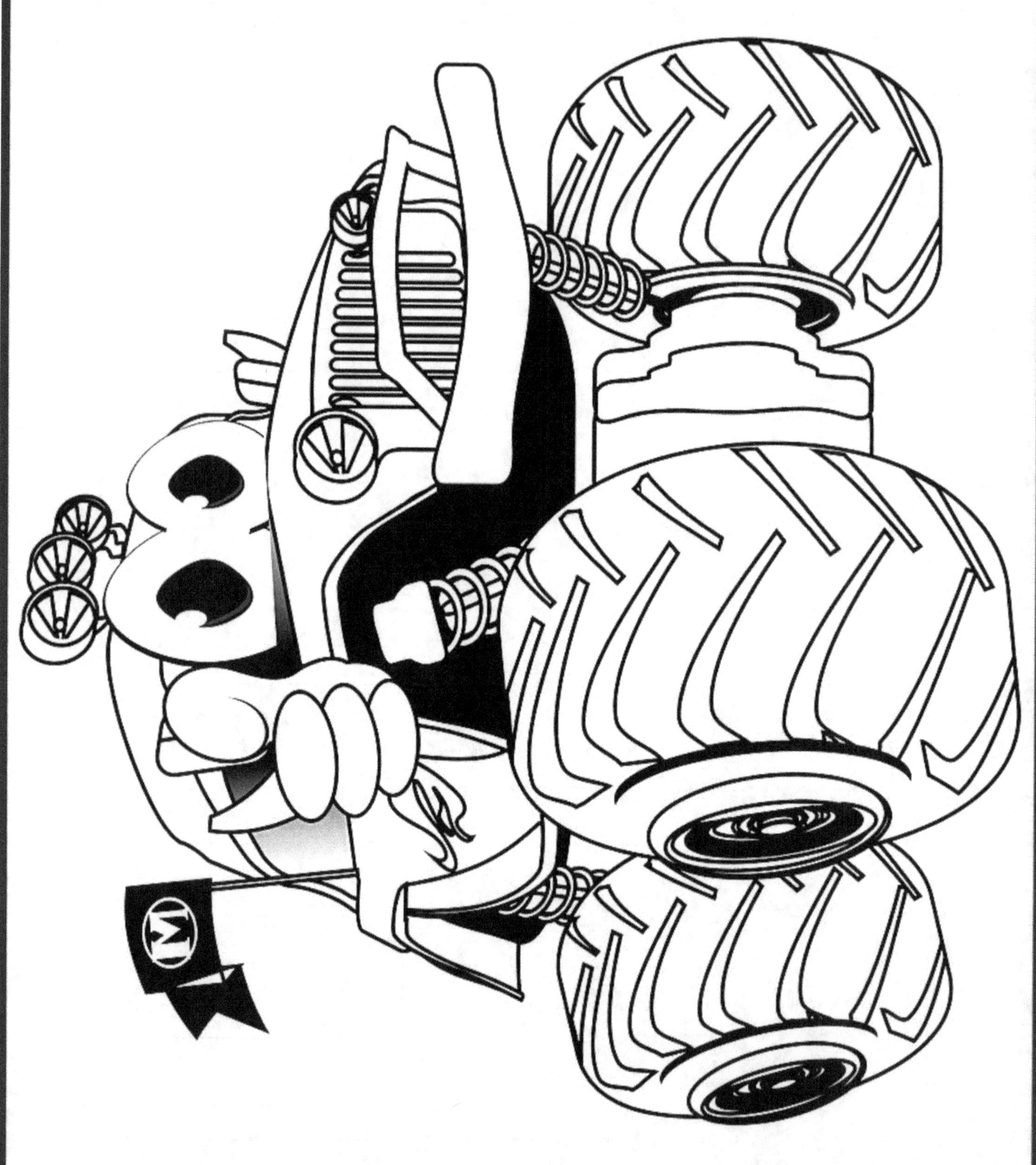

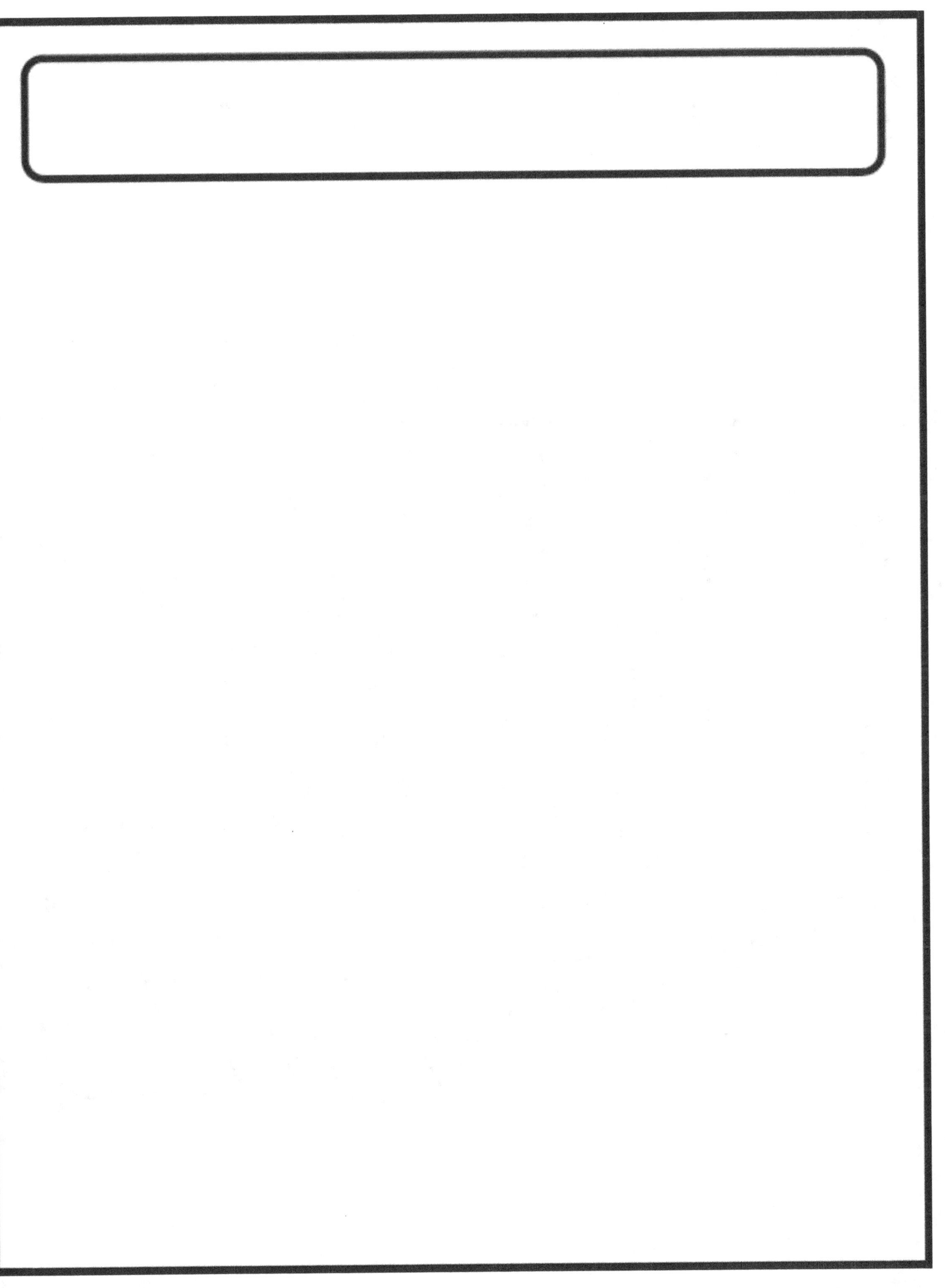

MONSTER TRUCK MALBUCH

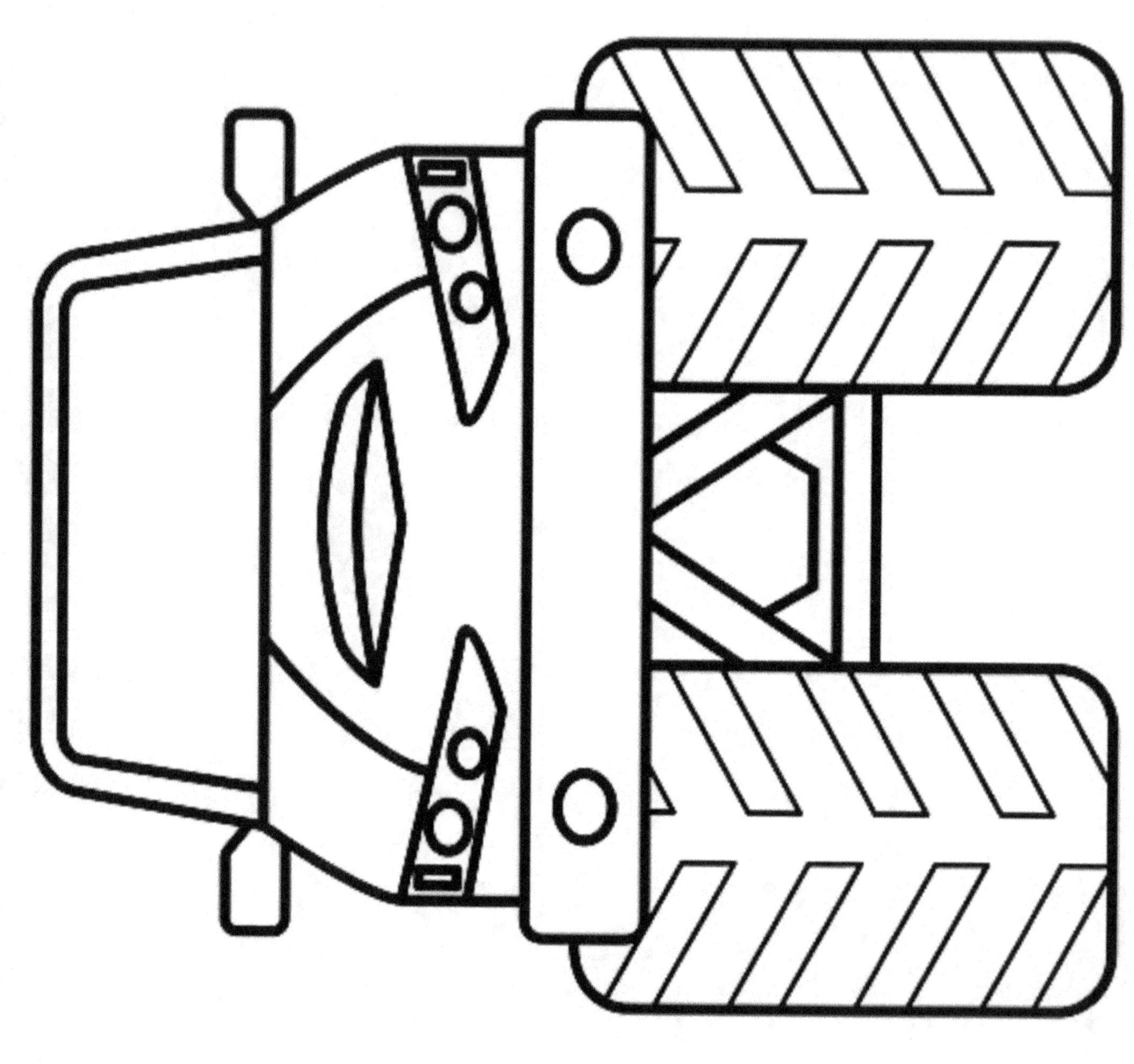

MONSTER TRUCK MALBUCH

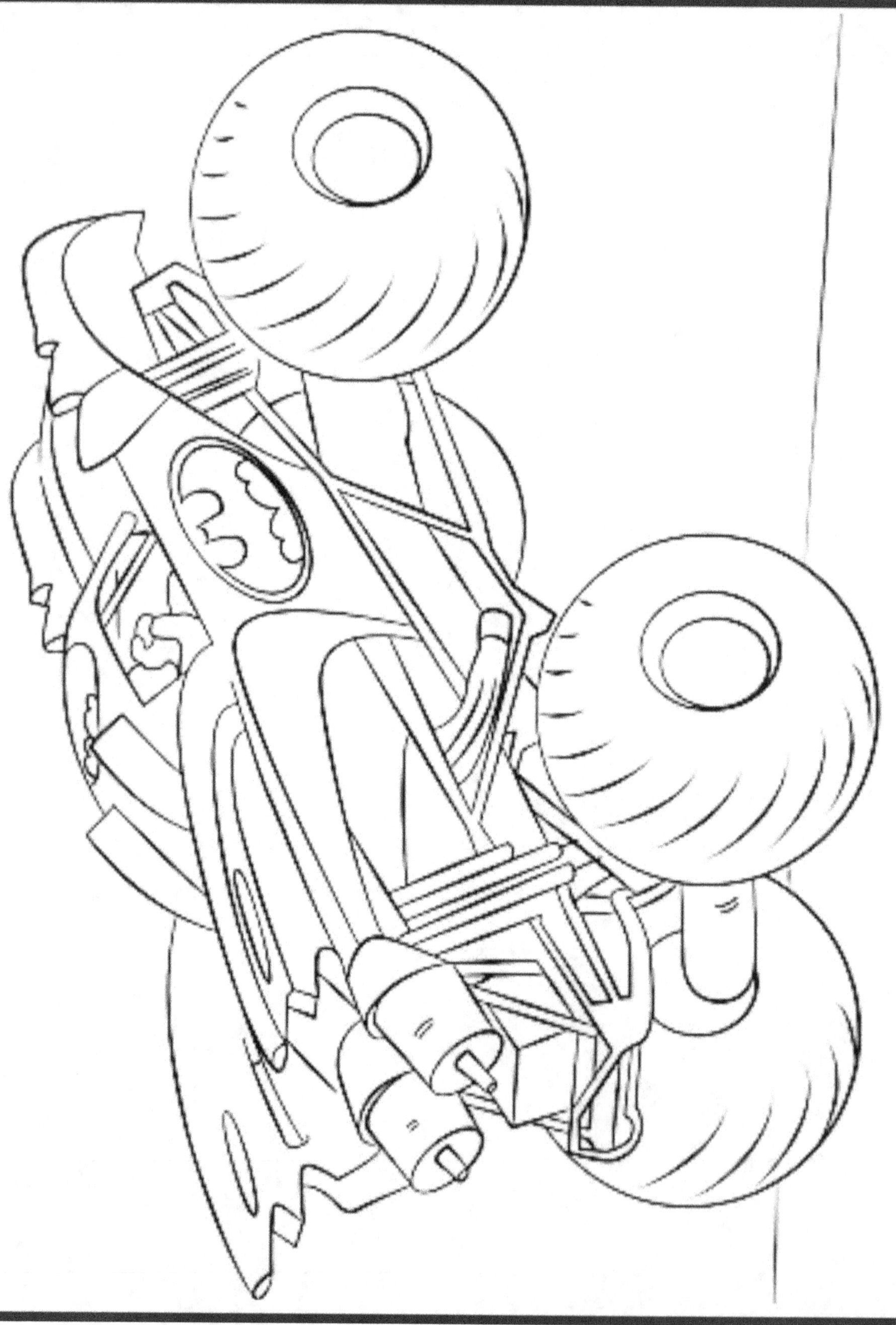

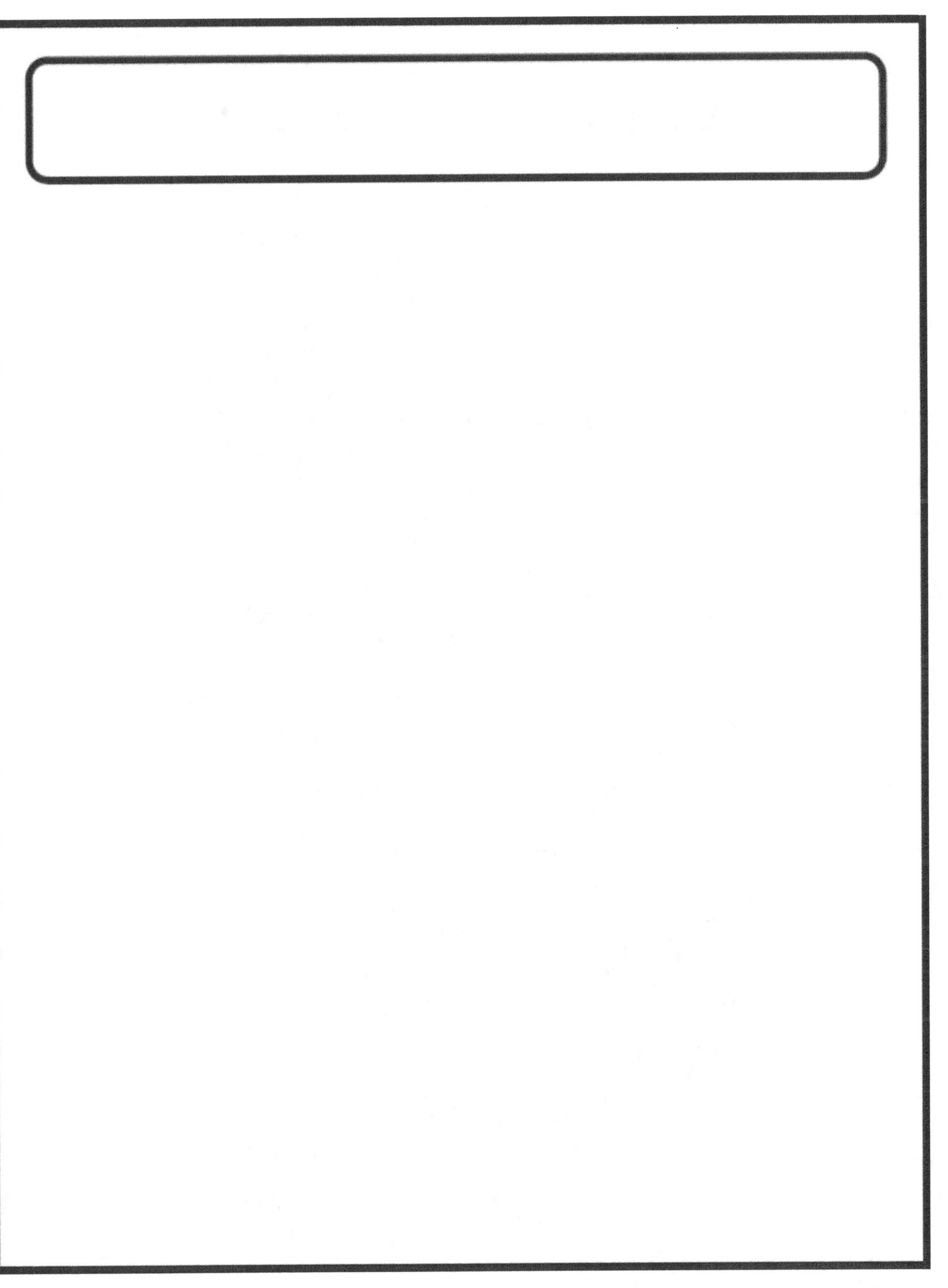

MONSTER TRUCK MALBUCH

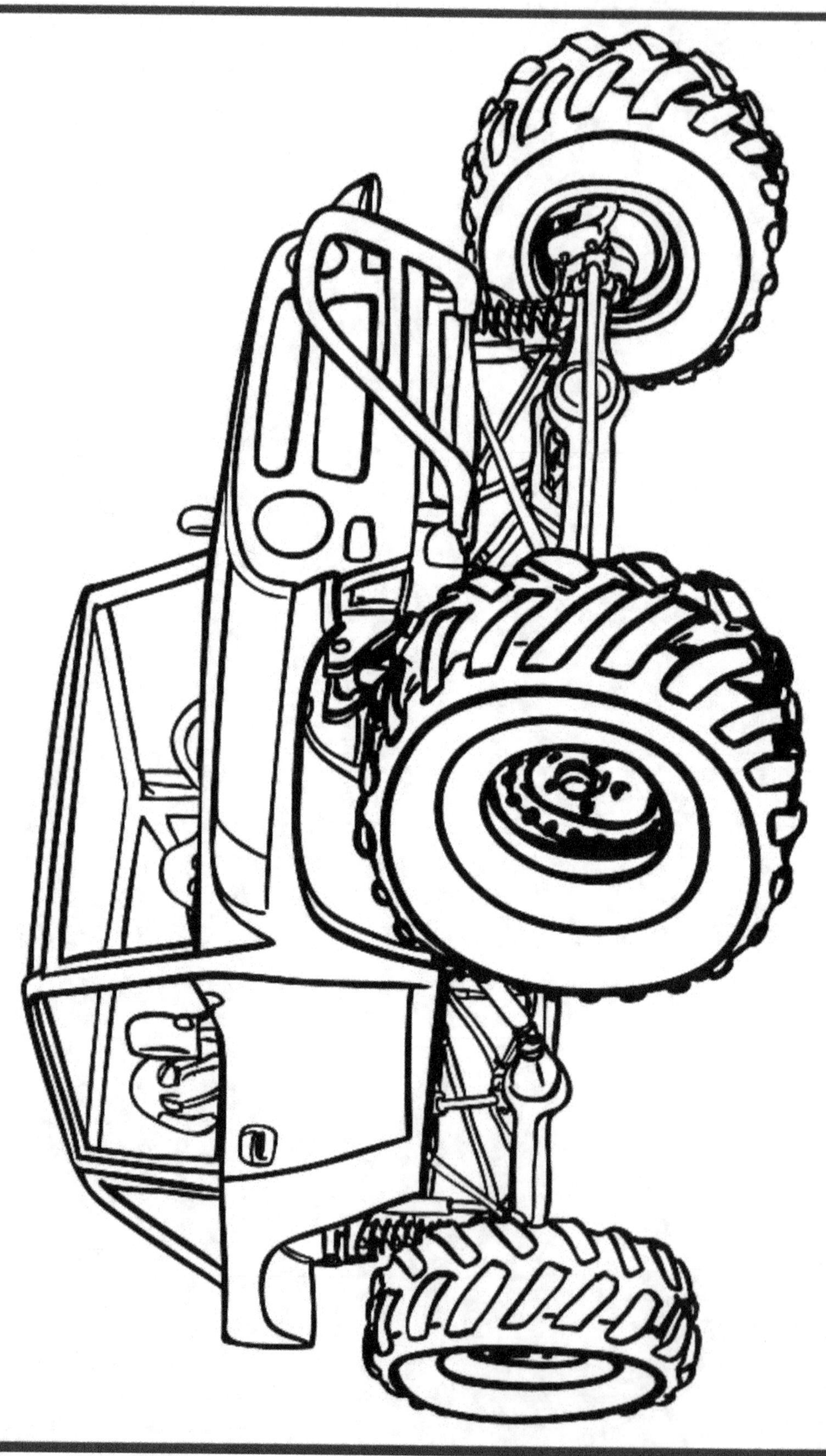

MONSTER TRUCK MALBUCH

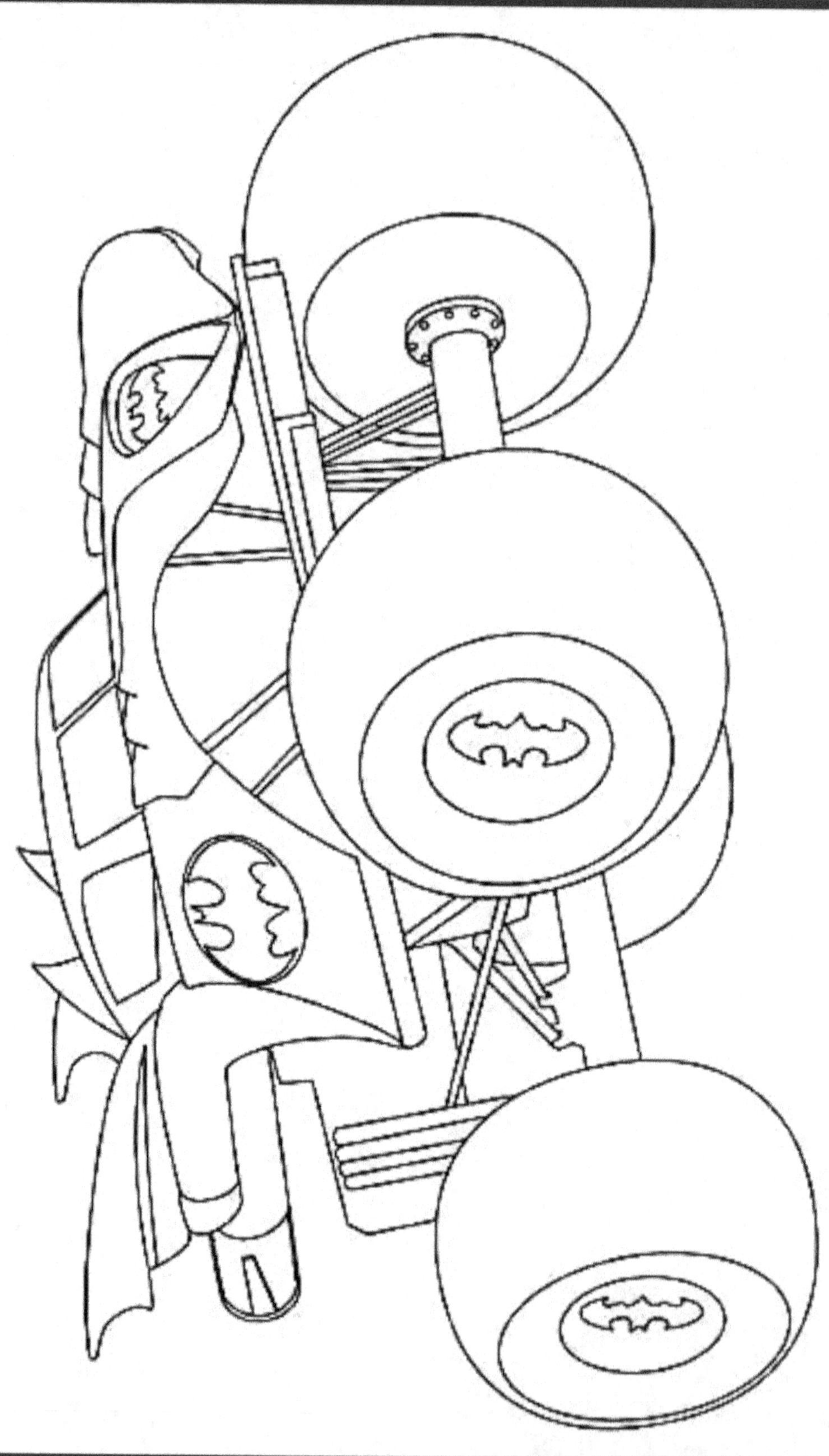

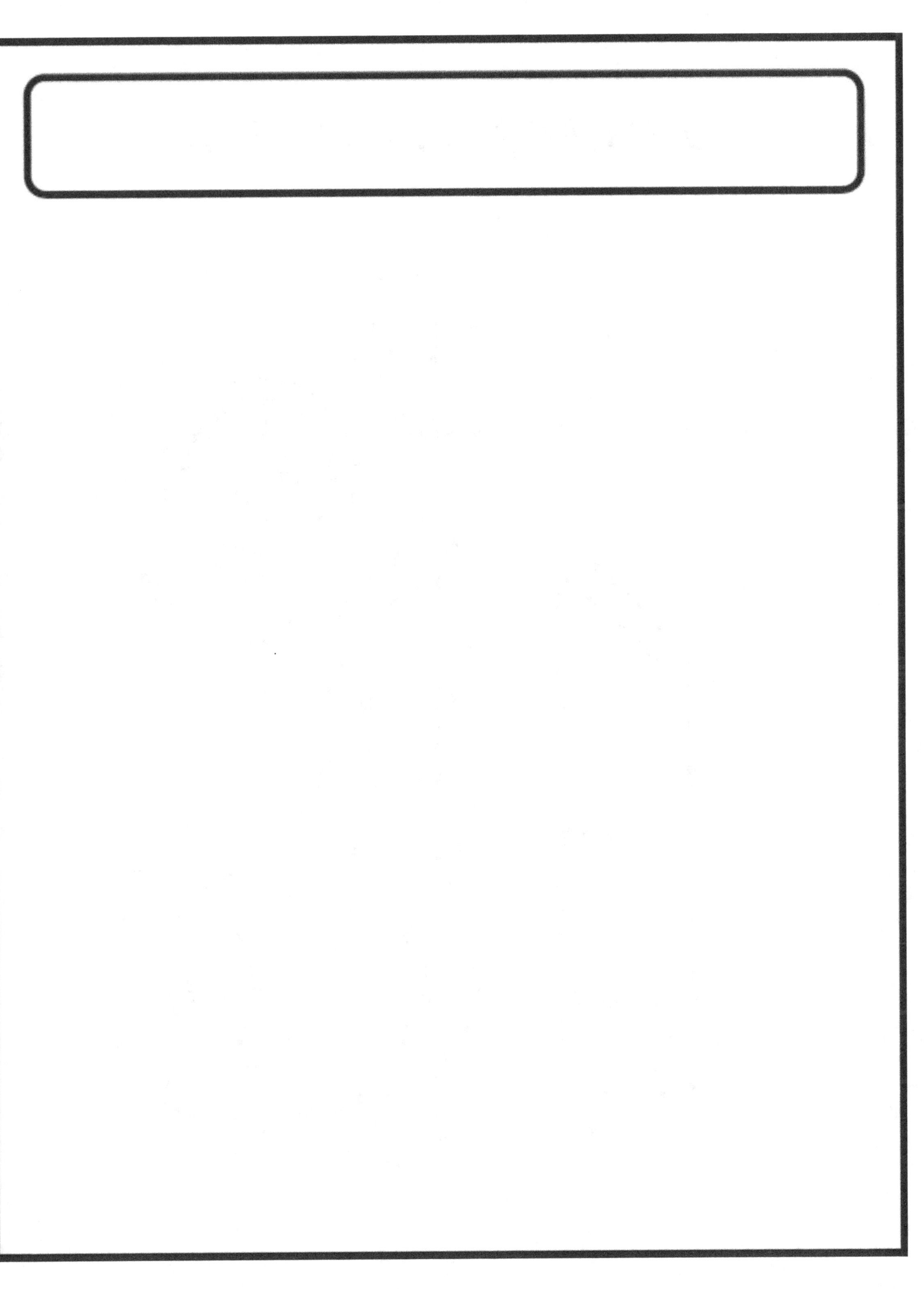

MONSTER TRUCK MALBUCH

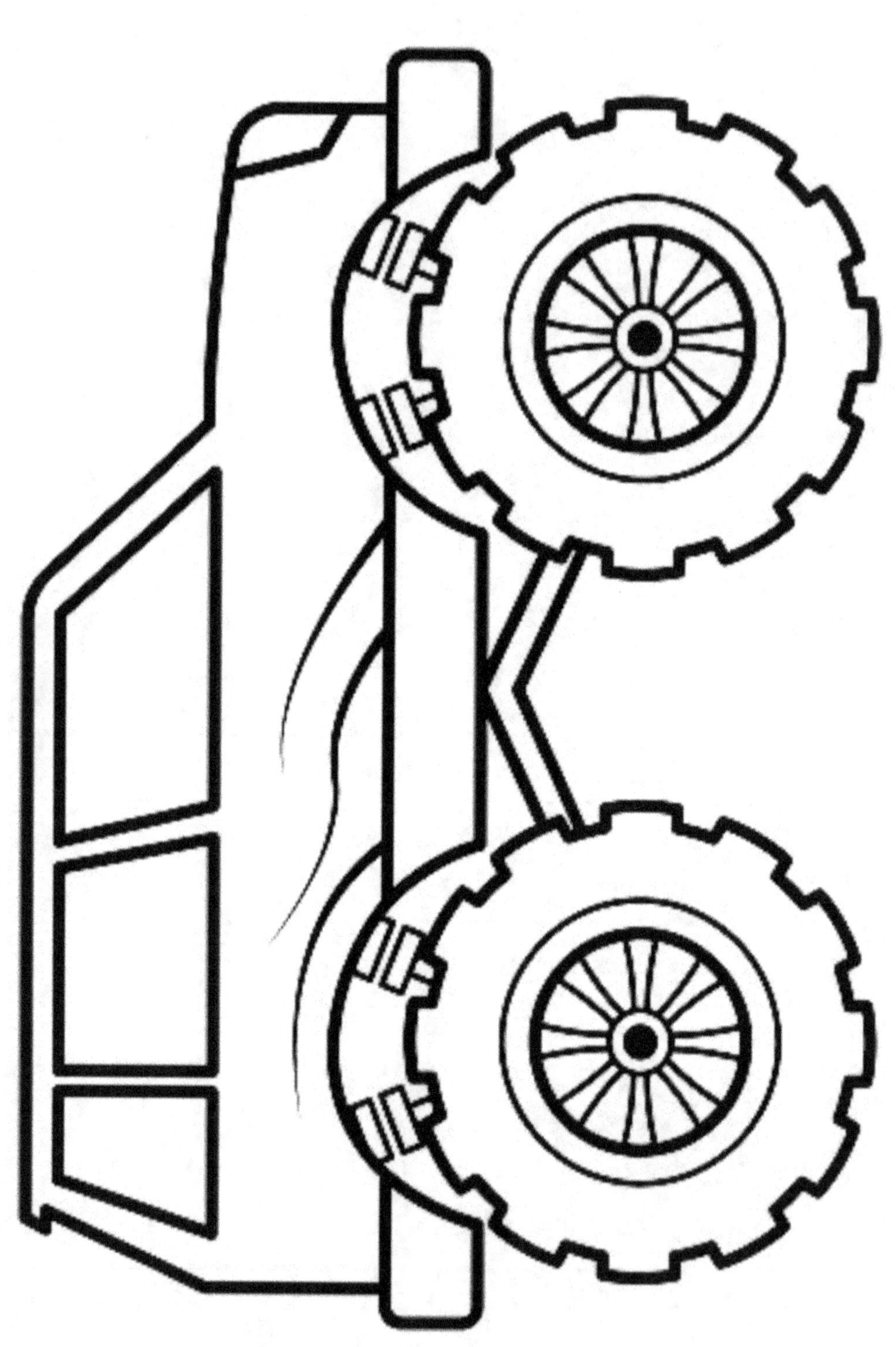

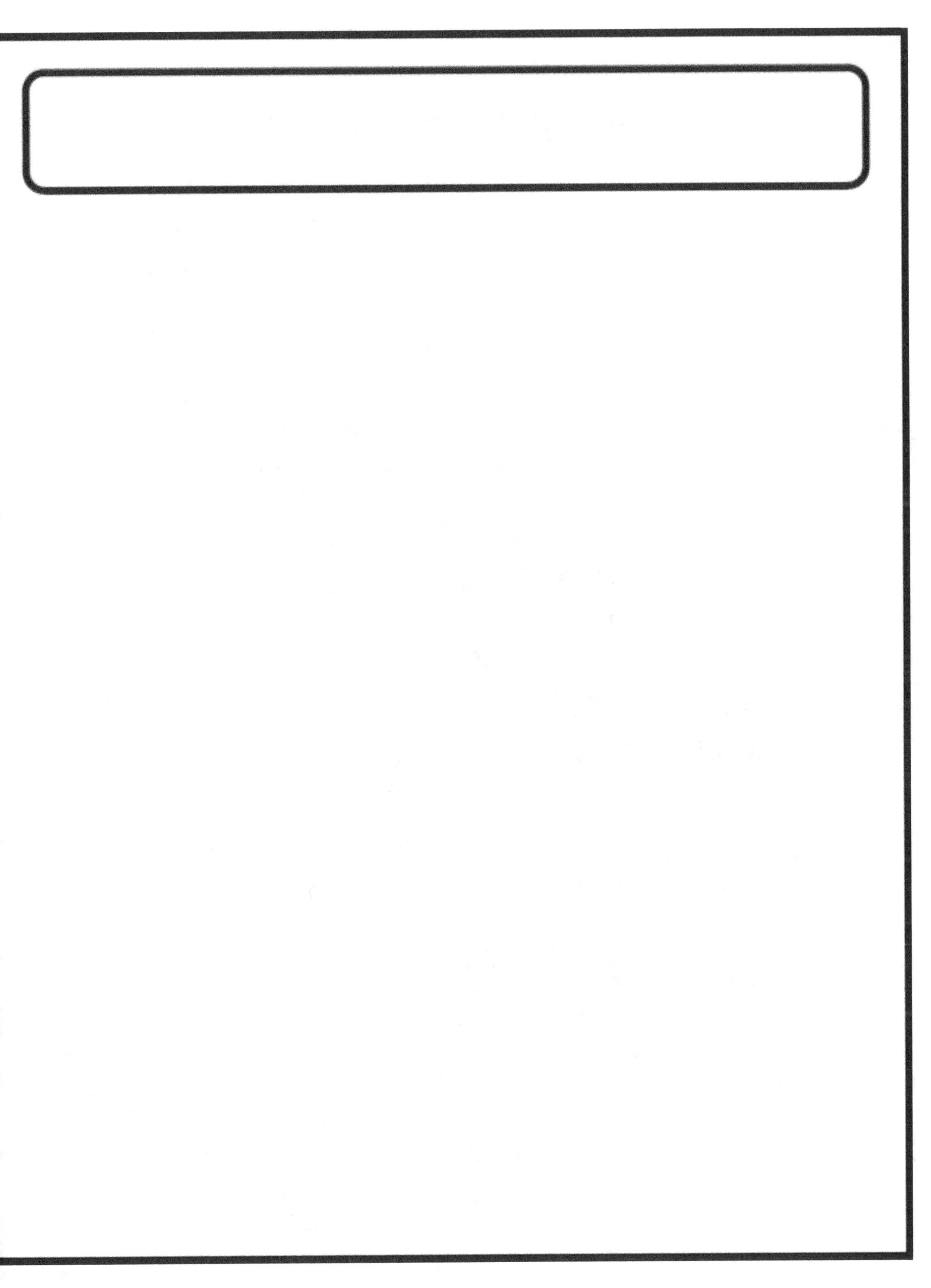

MONSTER TRUCK MALBUCH

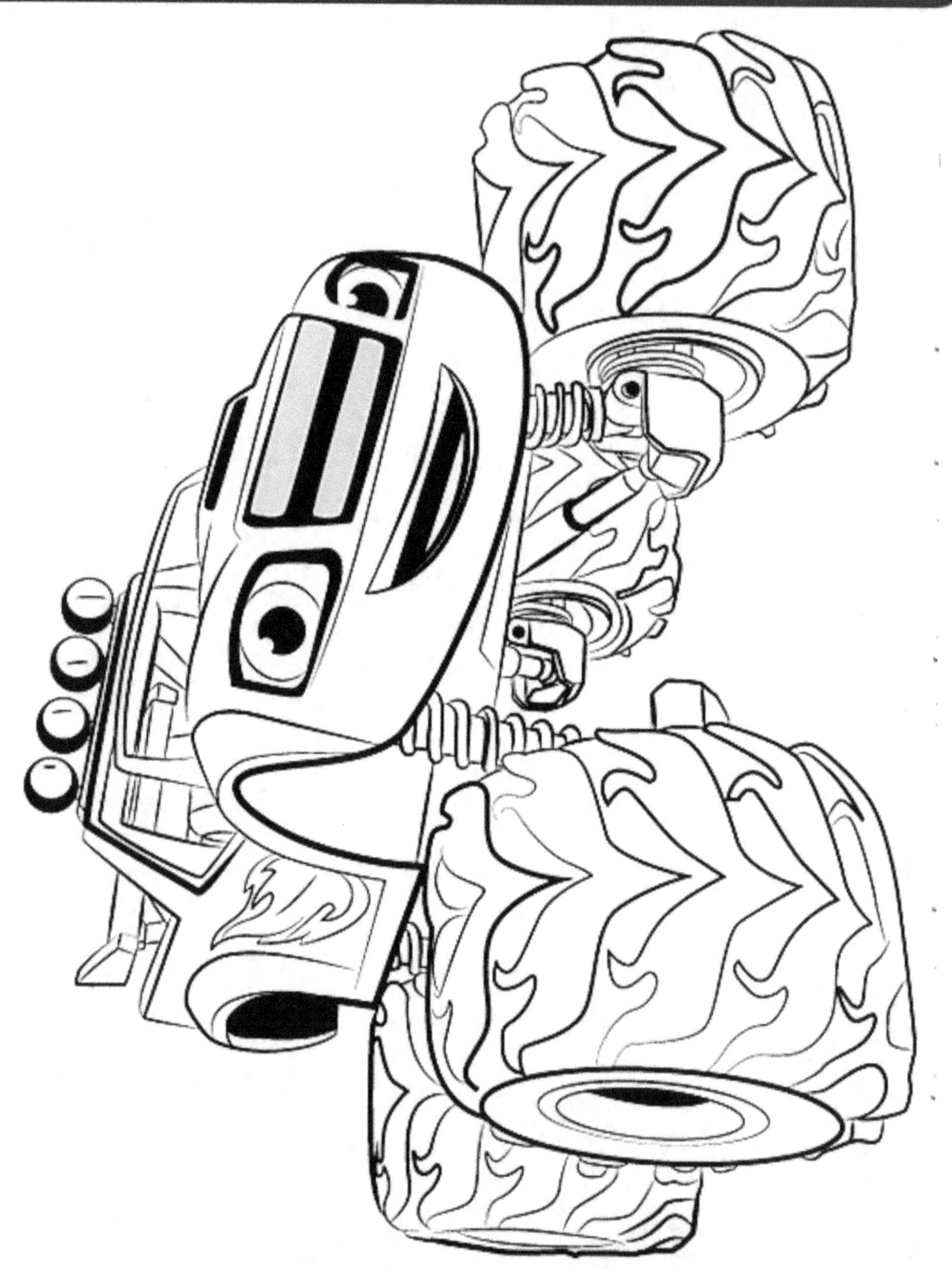

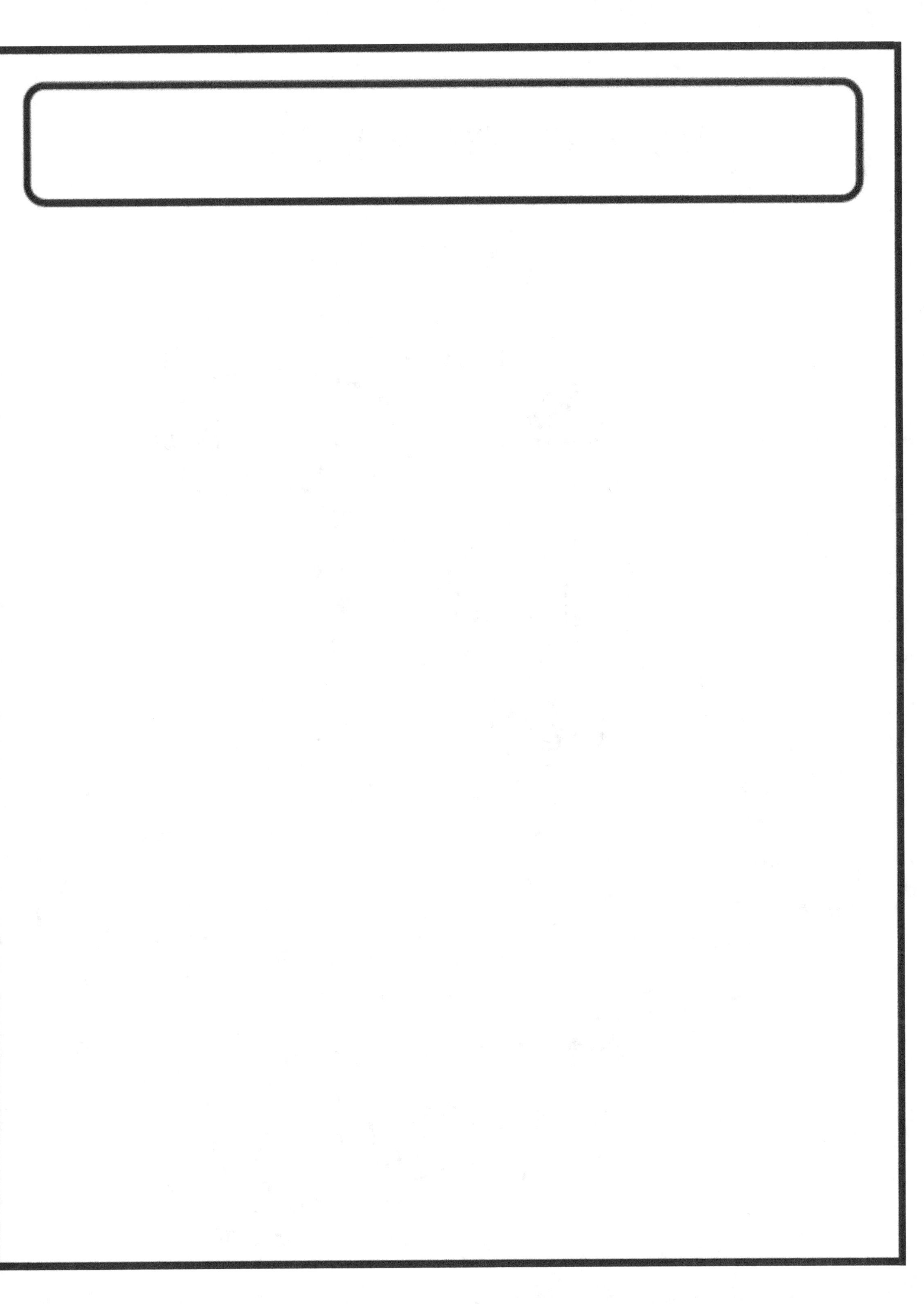

MONSTER TRUCK MALBUCH

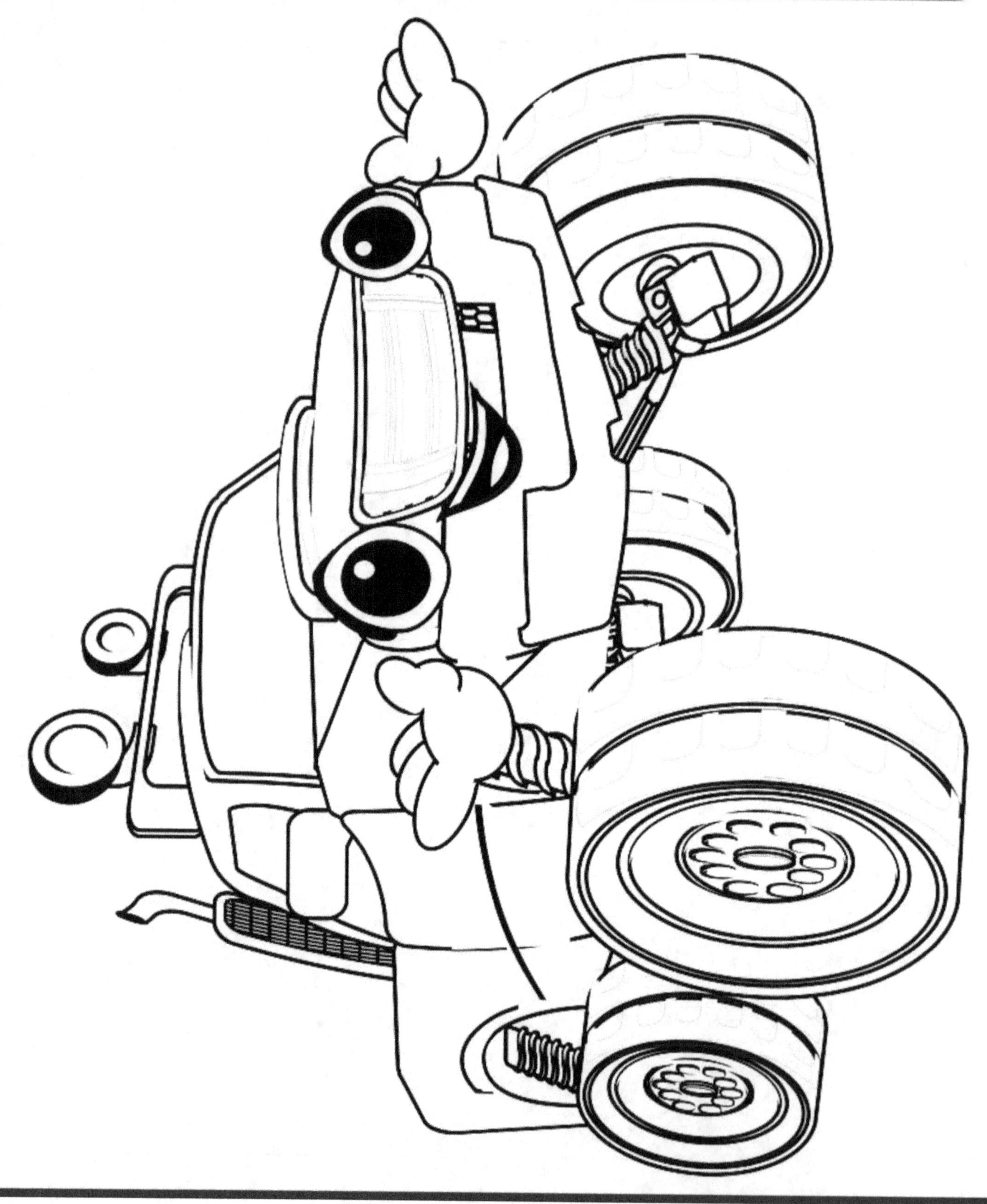

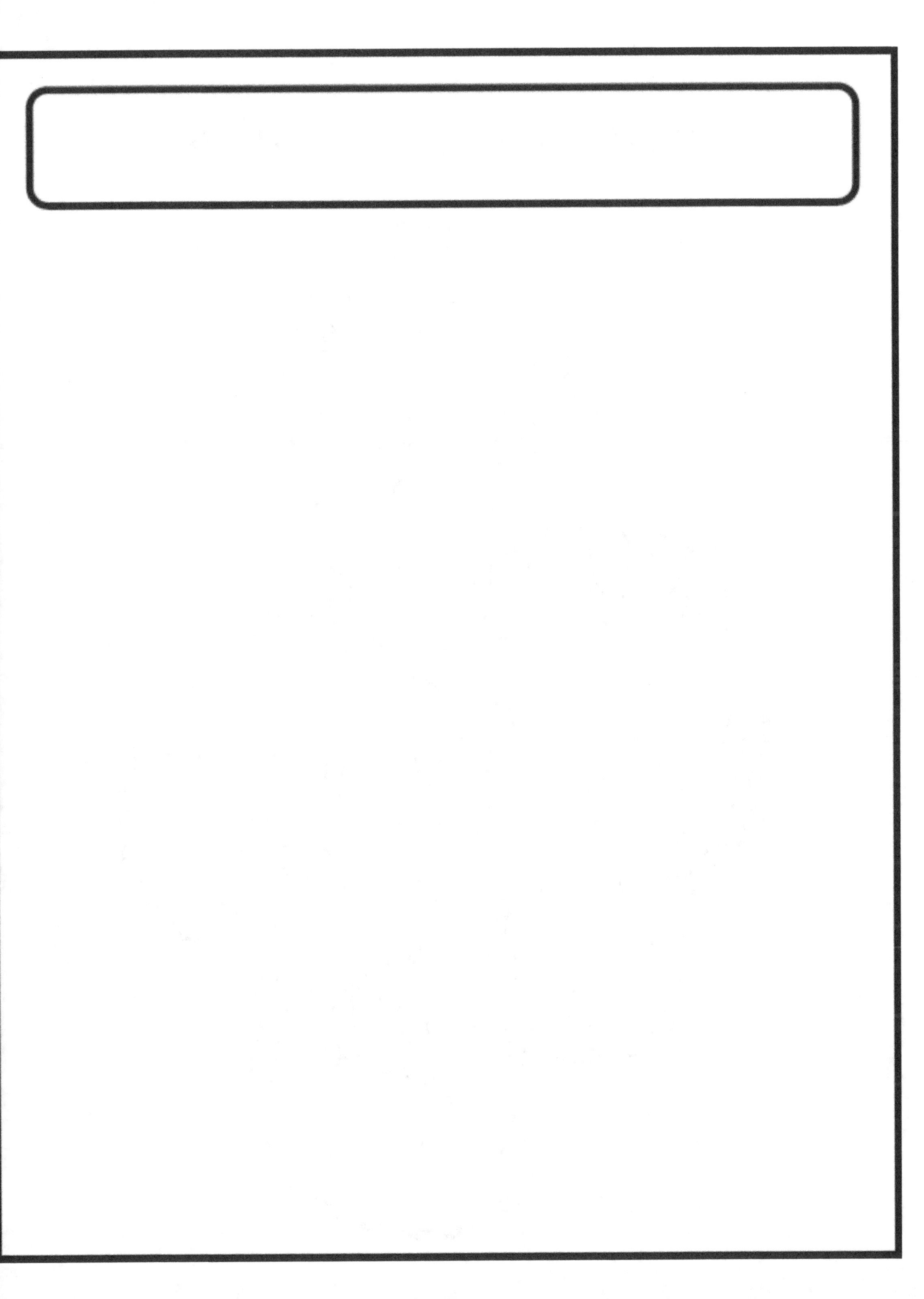

MONSTER TRUCK MALBUCH

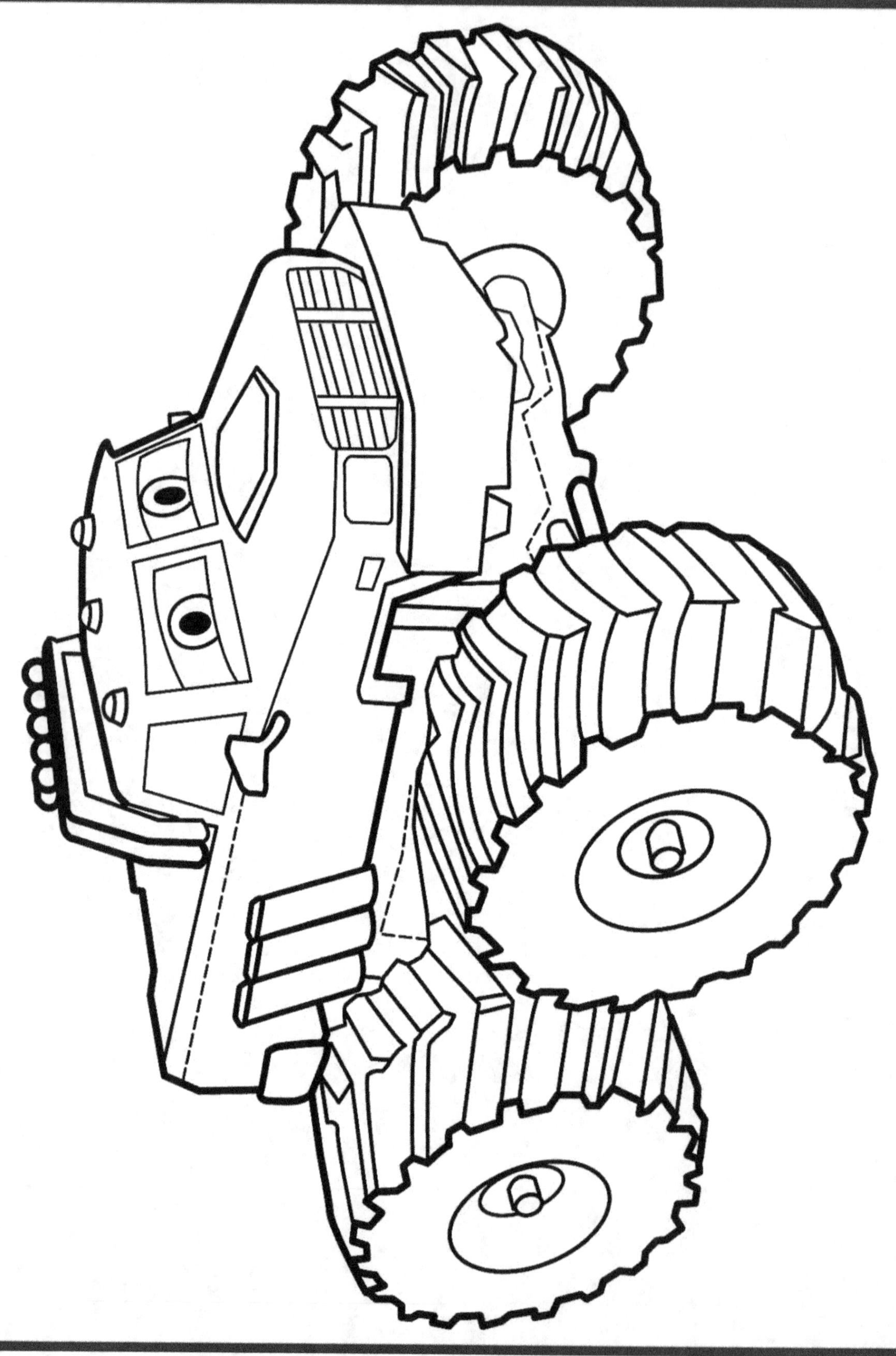

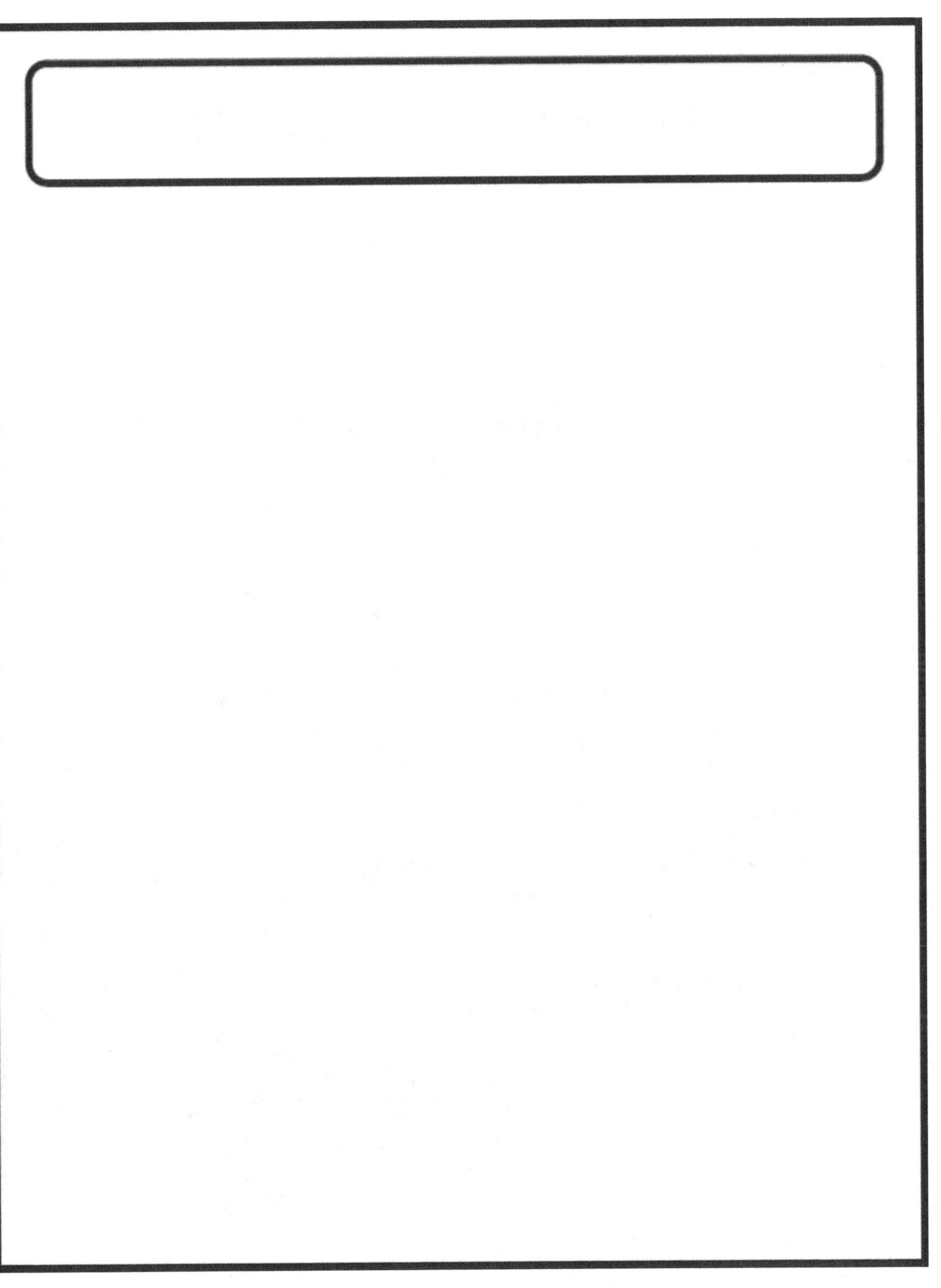

MONSTER TRUCK MALBUCH

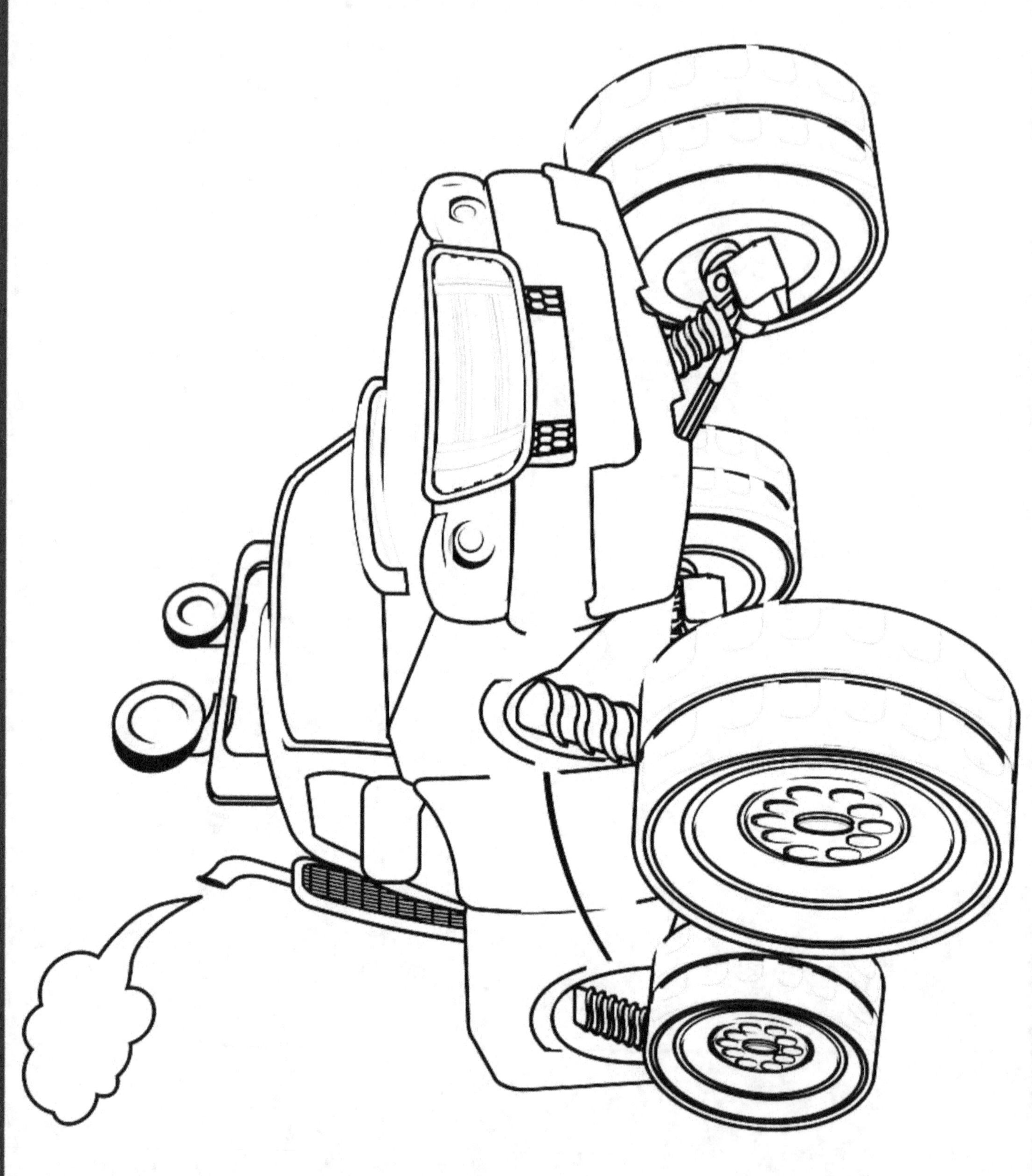

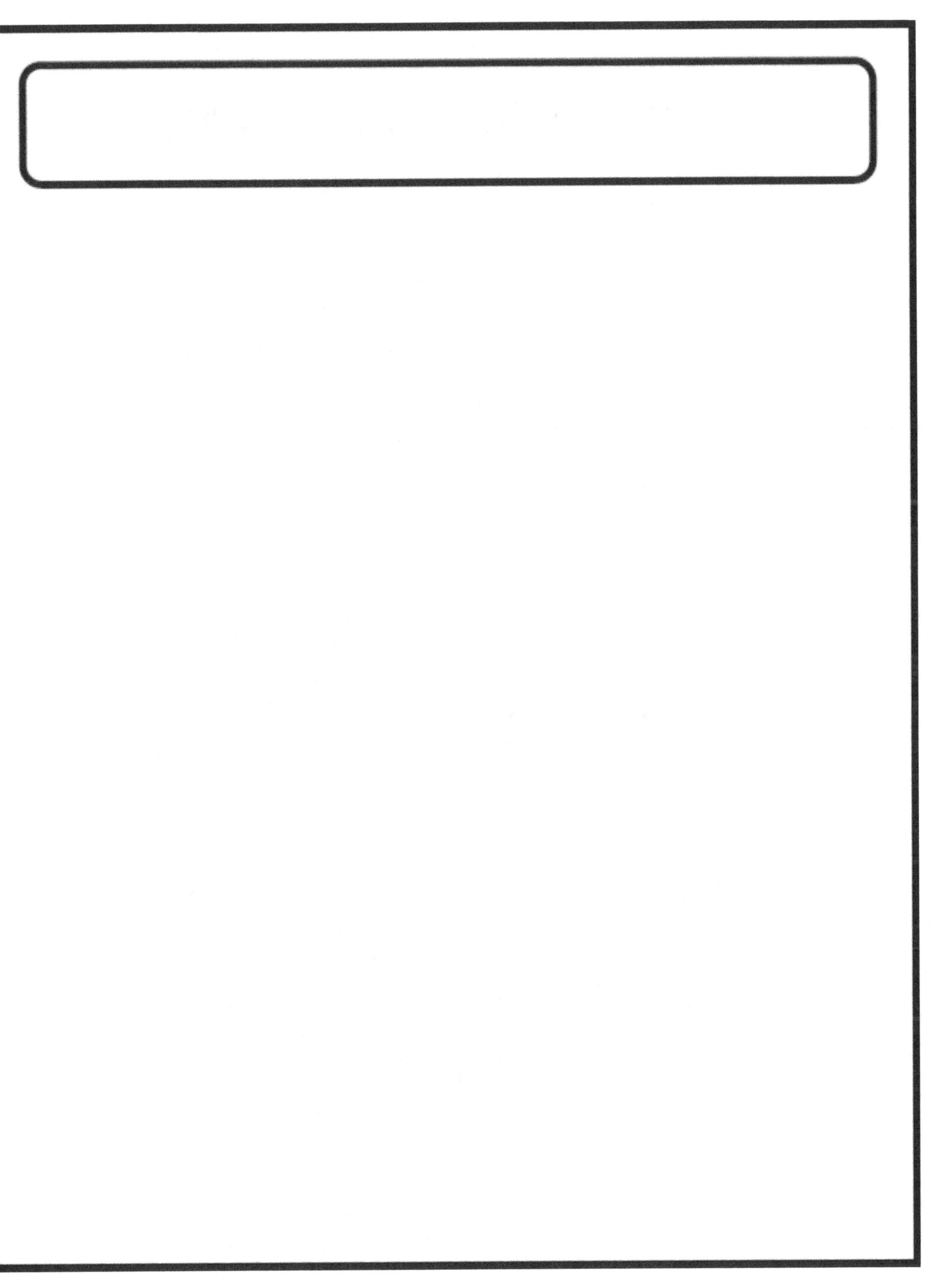

MONSTER TRUCK MALBUCH

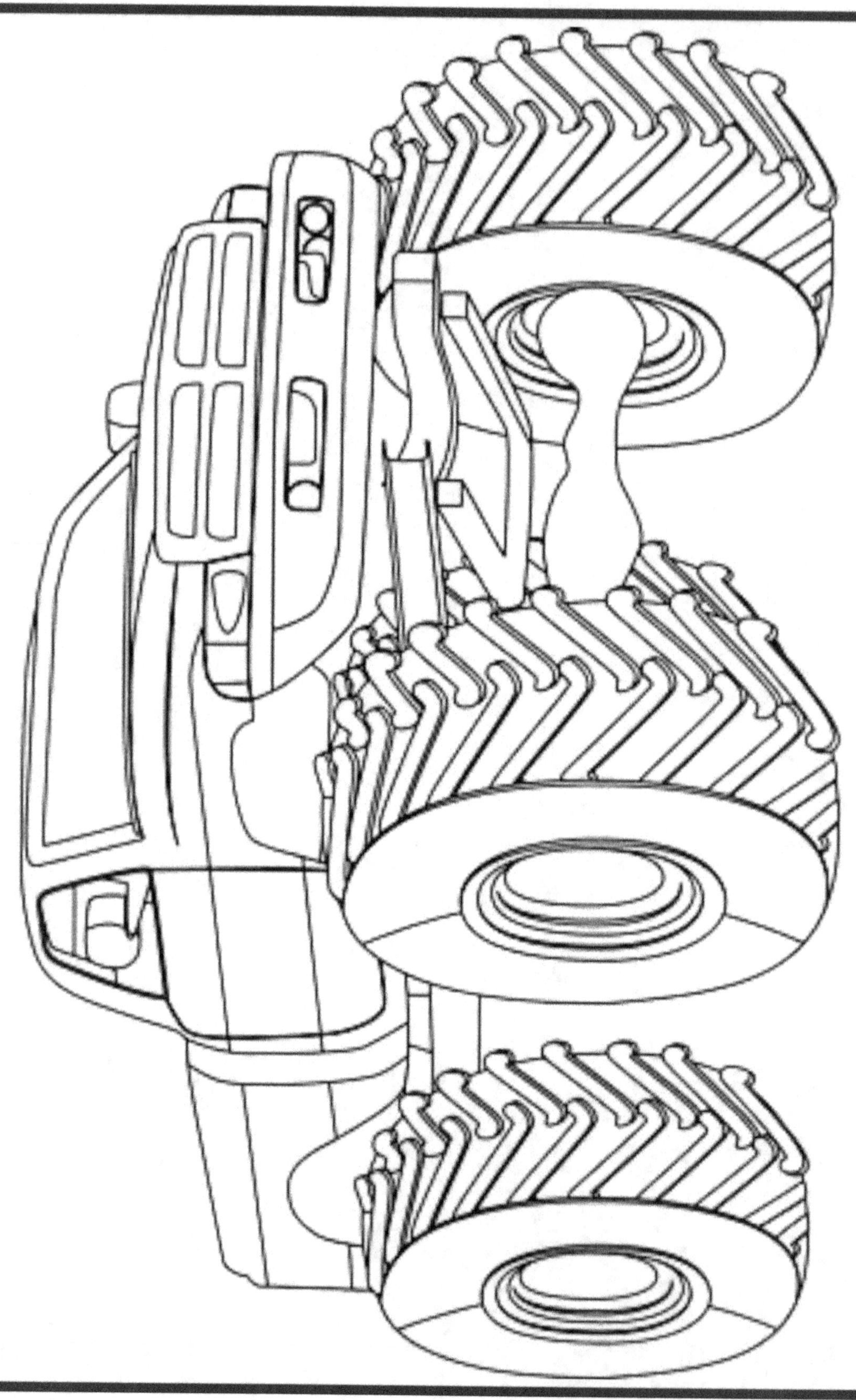

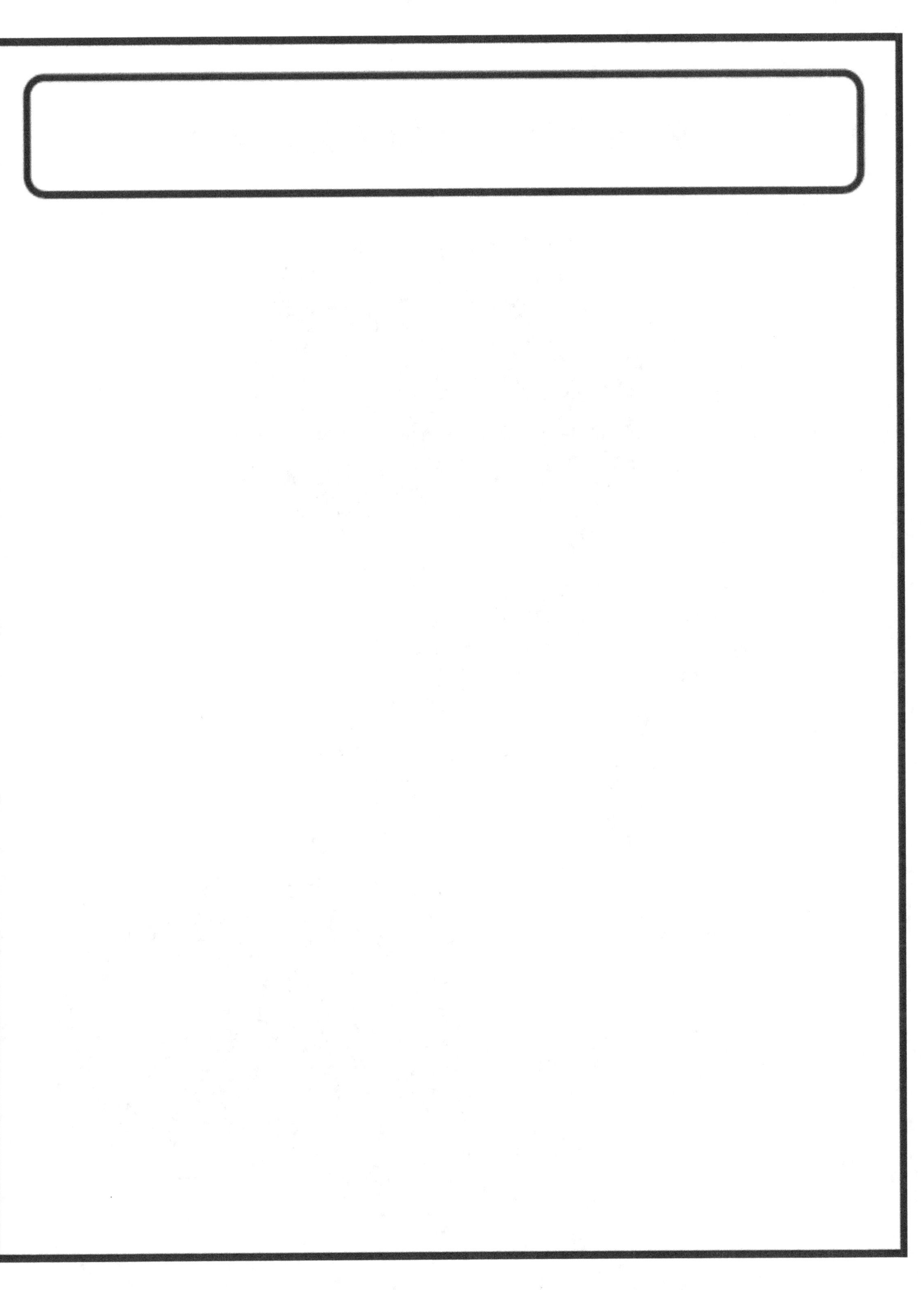

MONSTER TRUCK MALBUCH

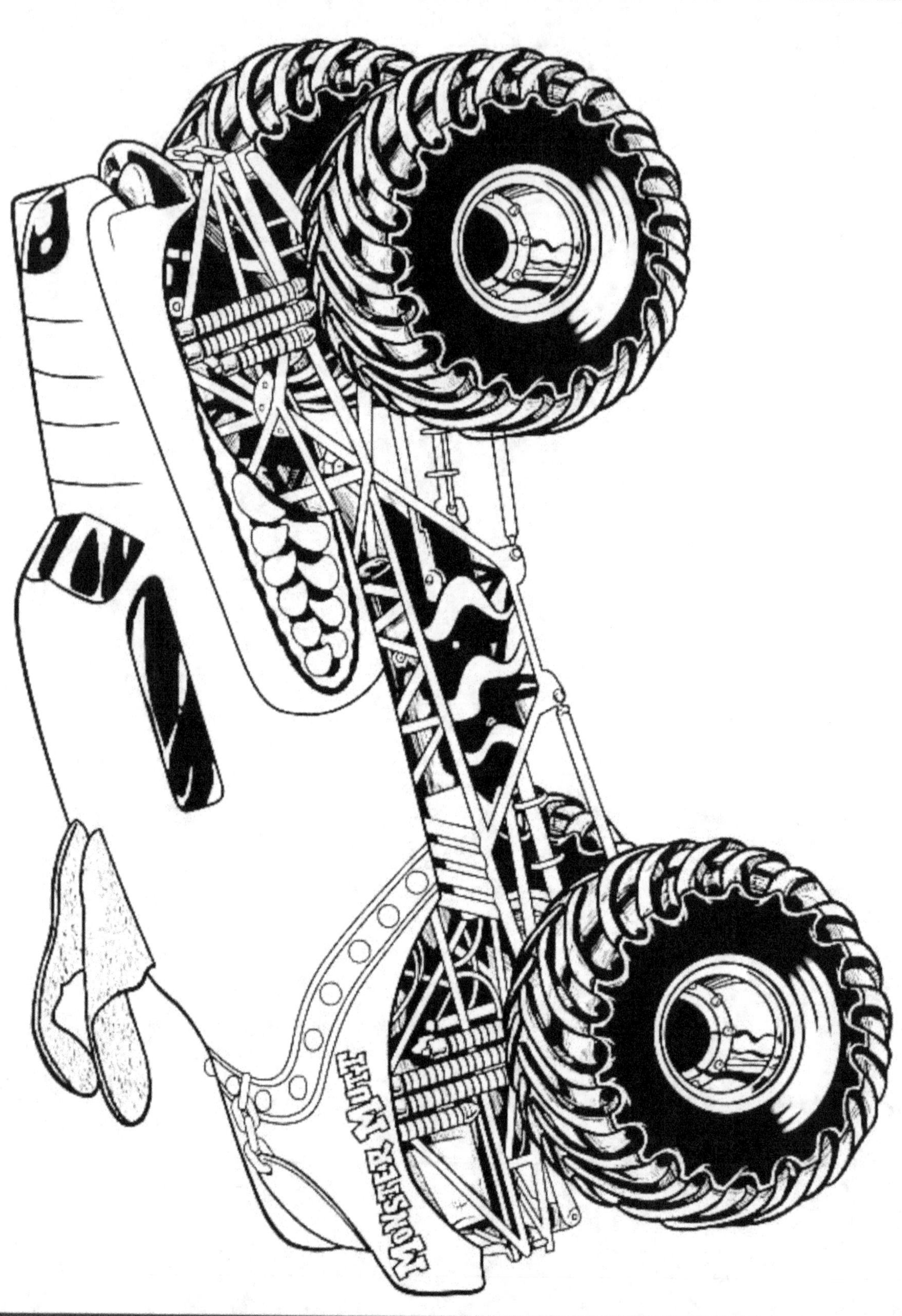

MONSTER TRUCK MALBUCH

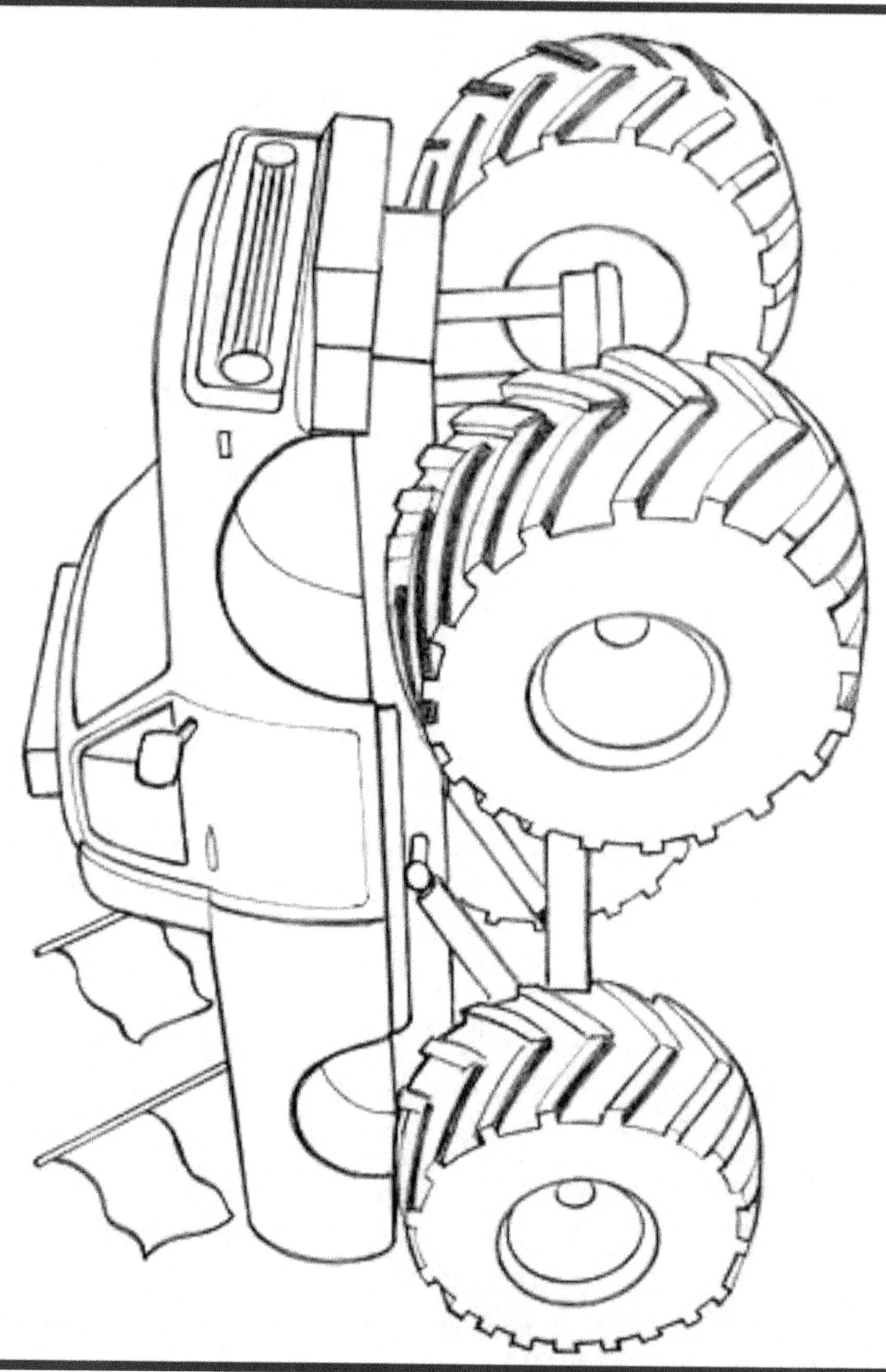

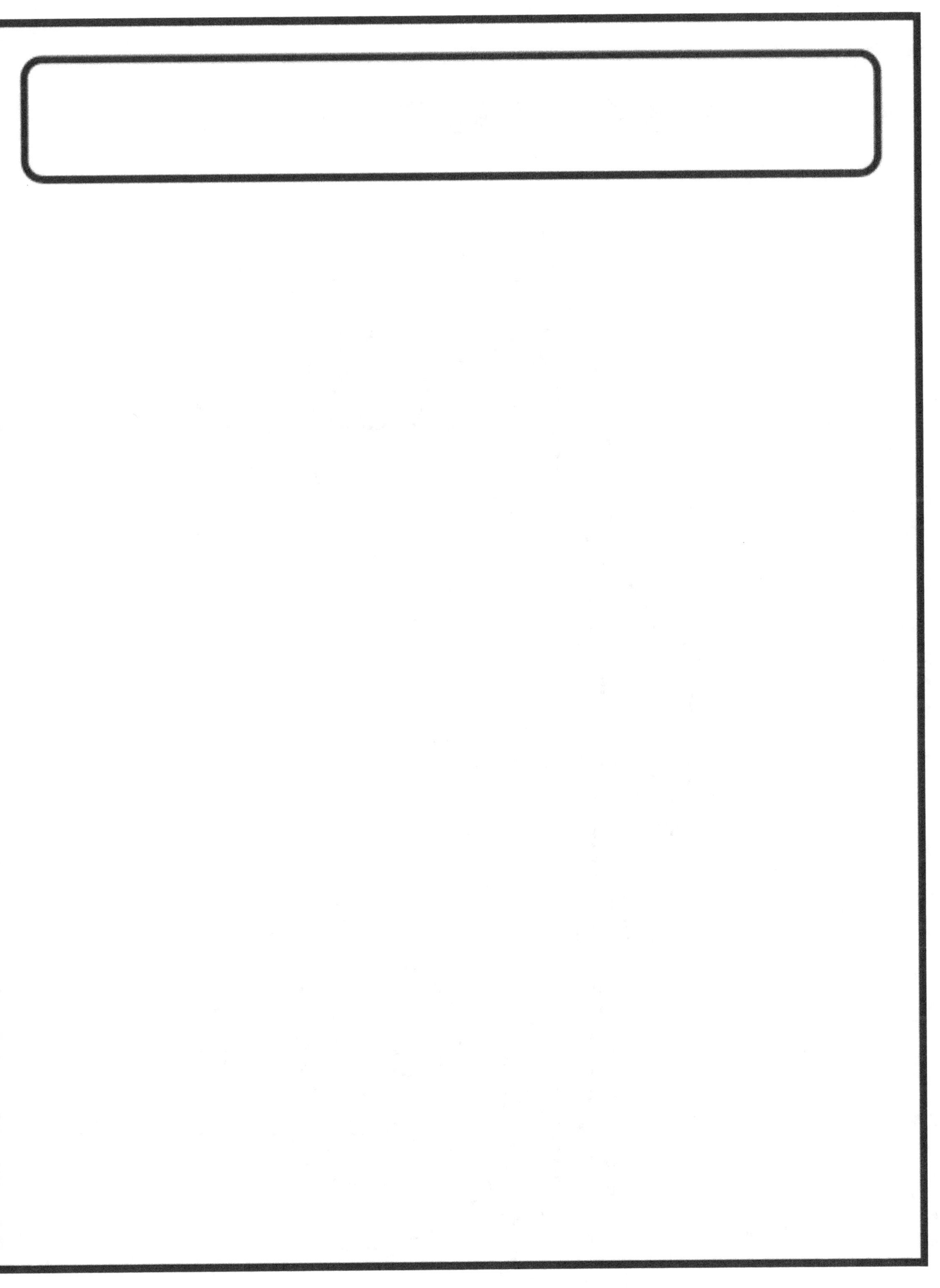

MONSTER TRUCK MALBUCH

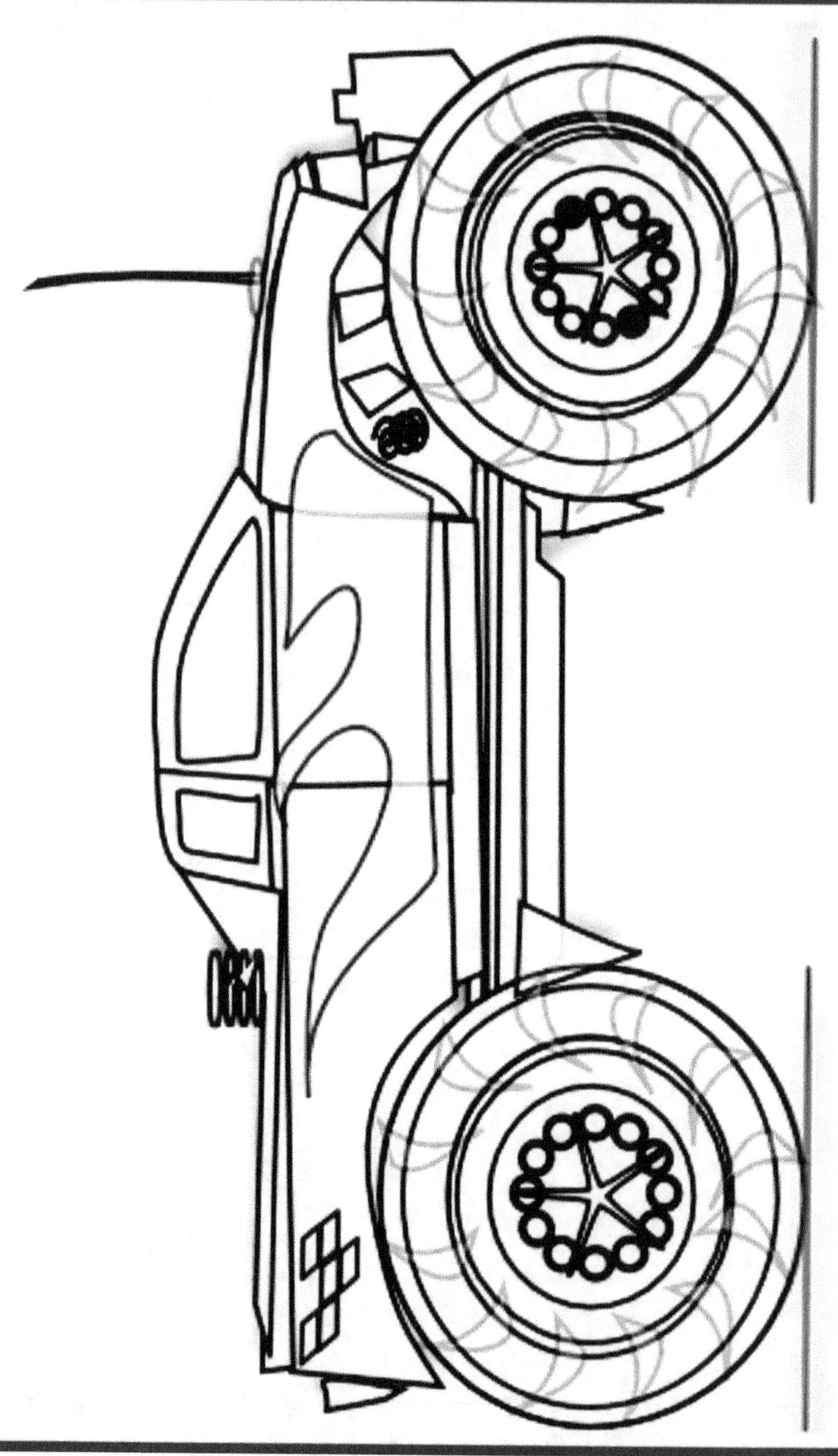

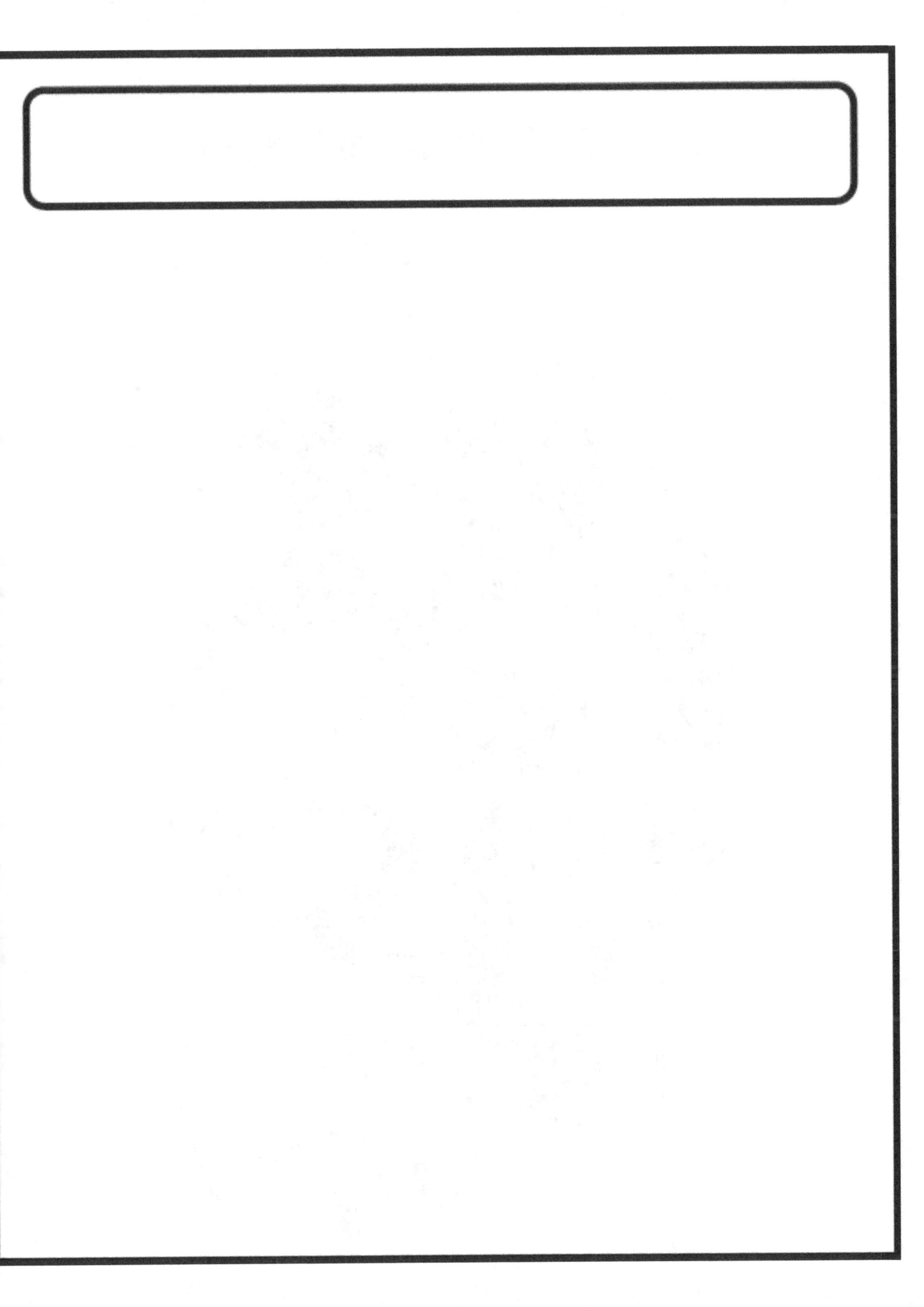

MONSTER TRUCK MALBUCH

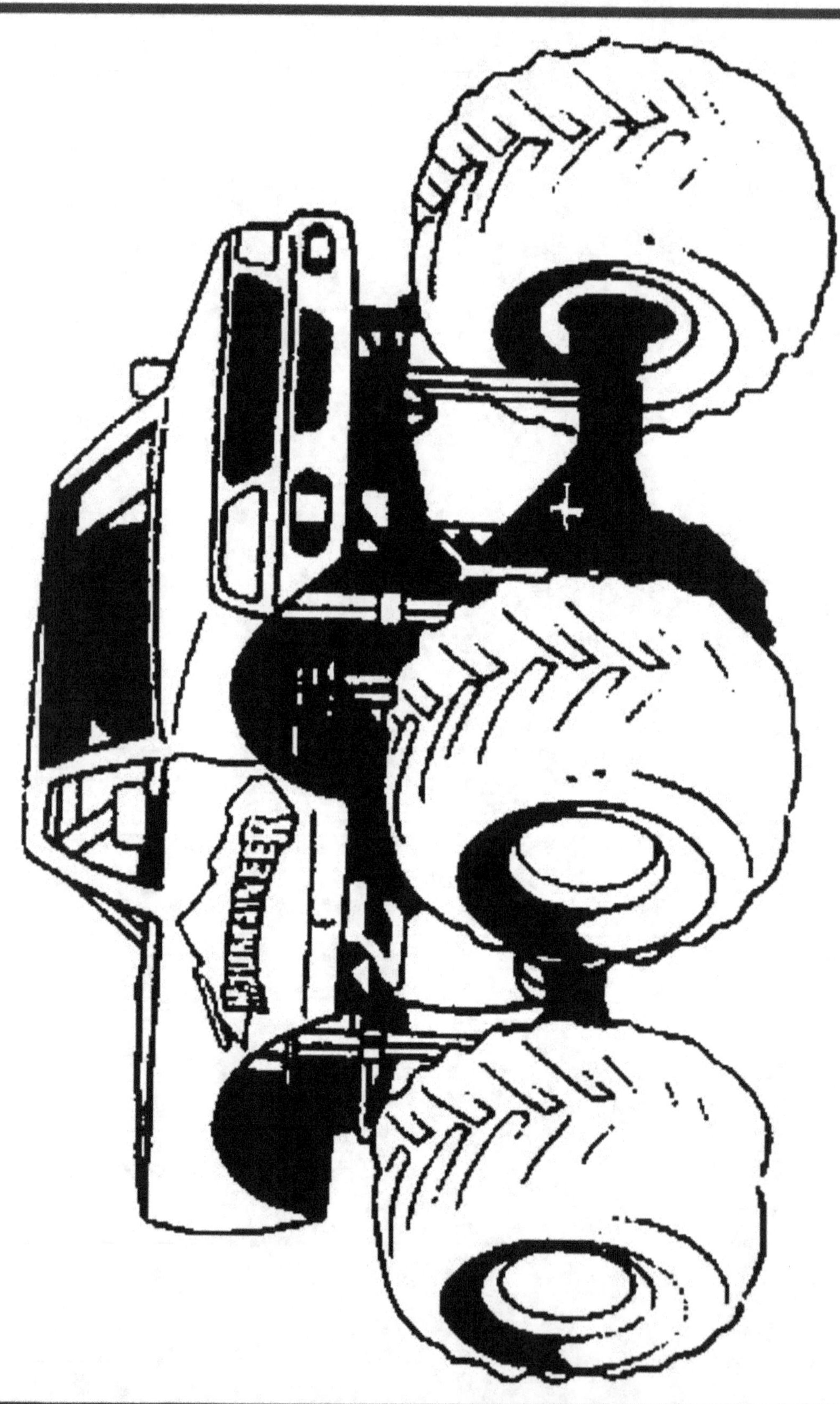

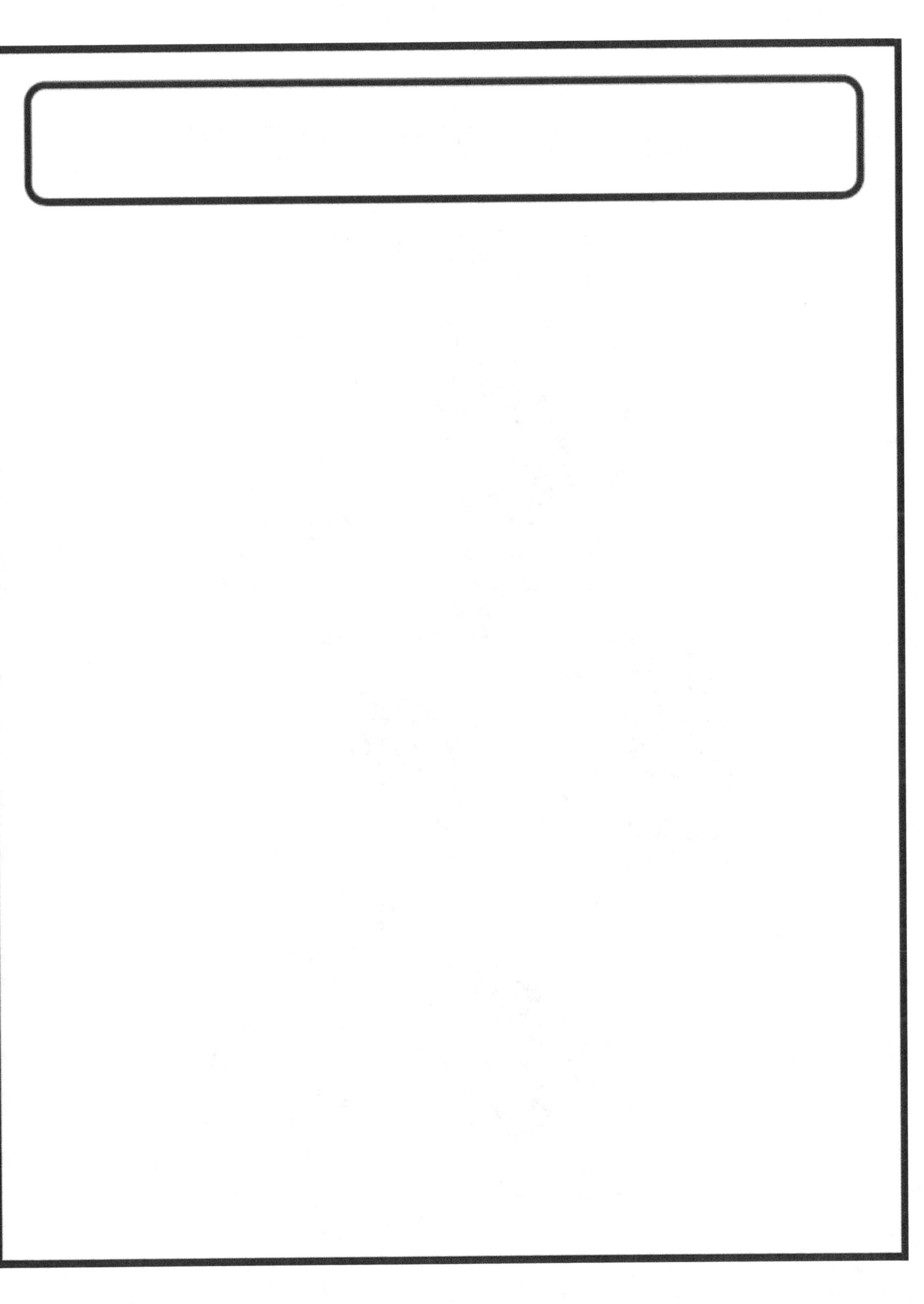

MONSTER TRUCK MALBUCH

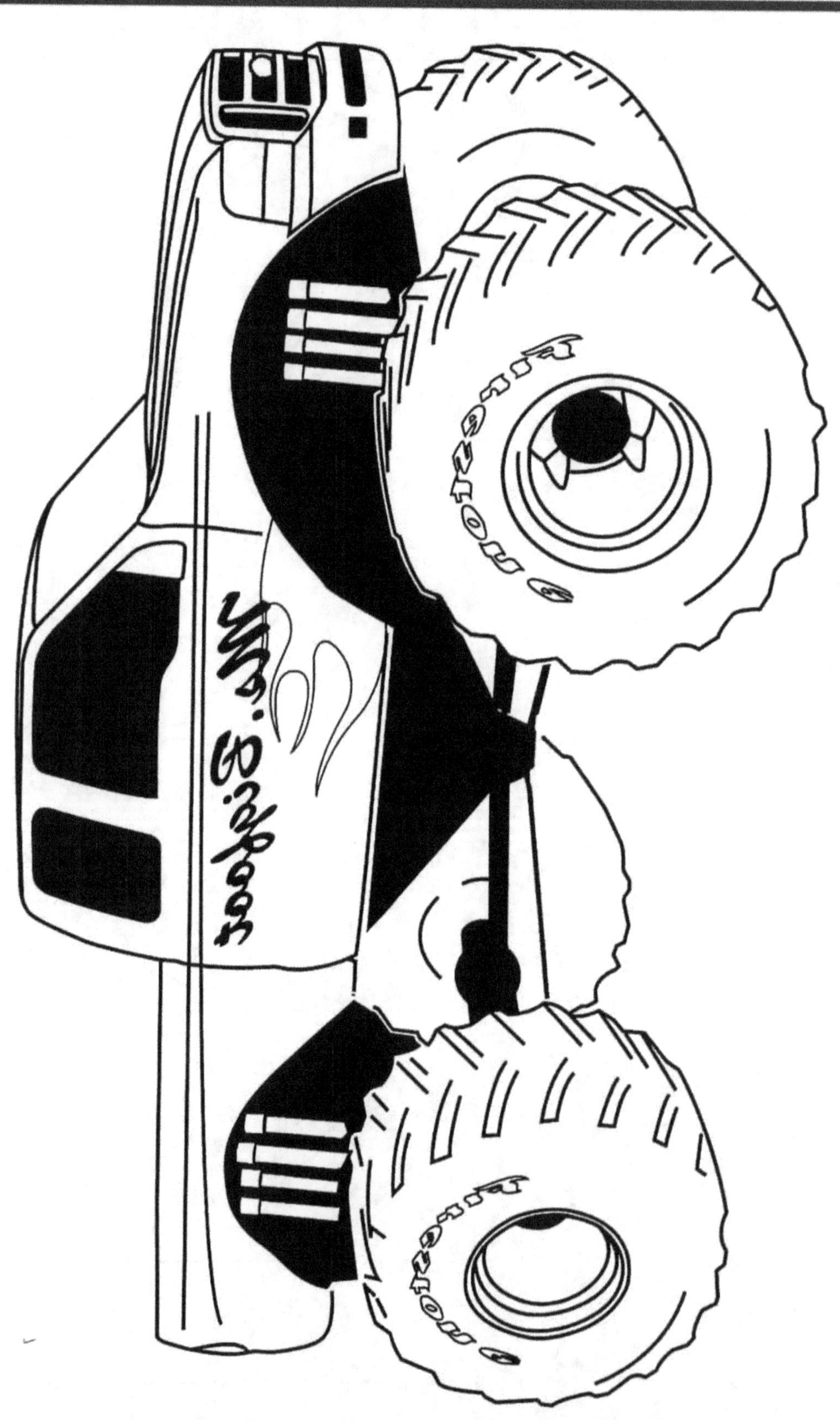

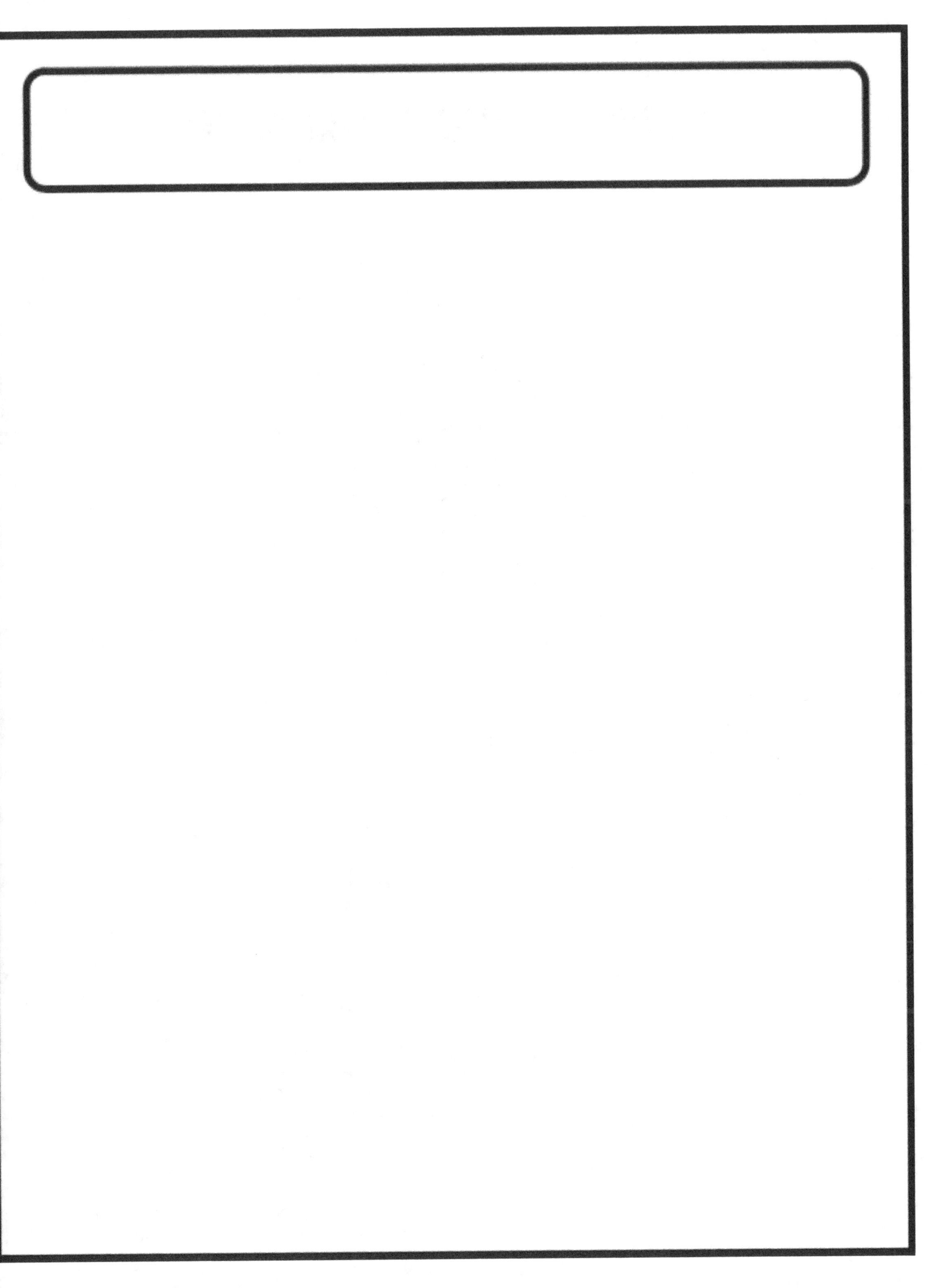

MONSTER TRUCK MALBUCH

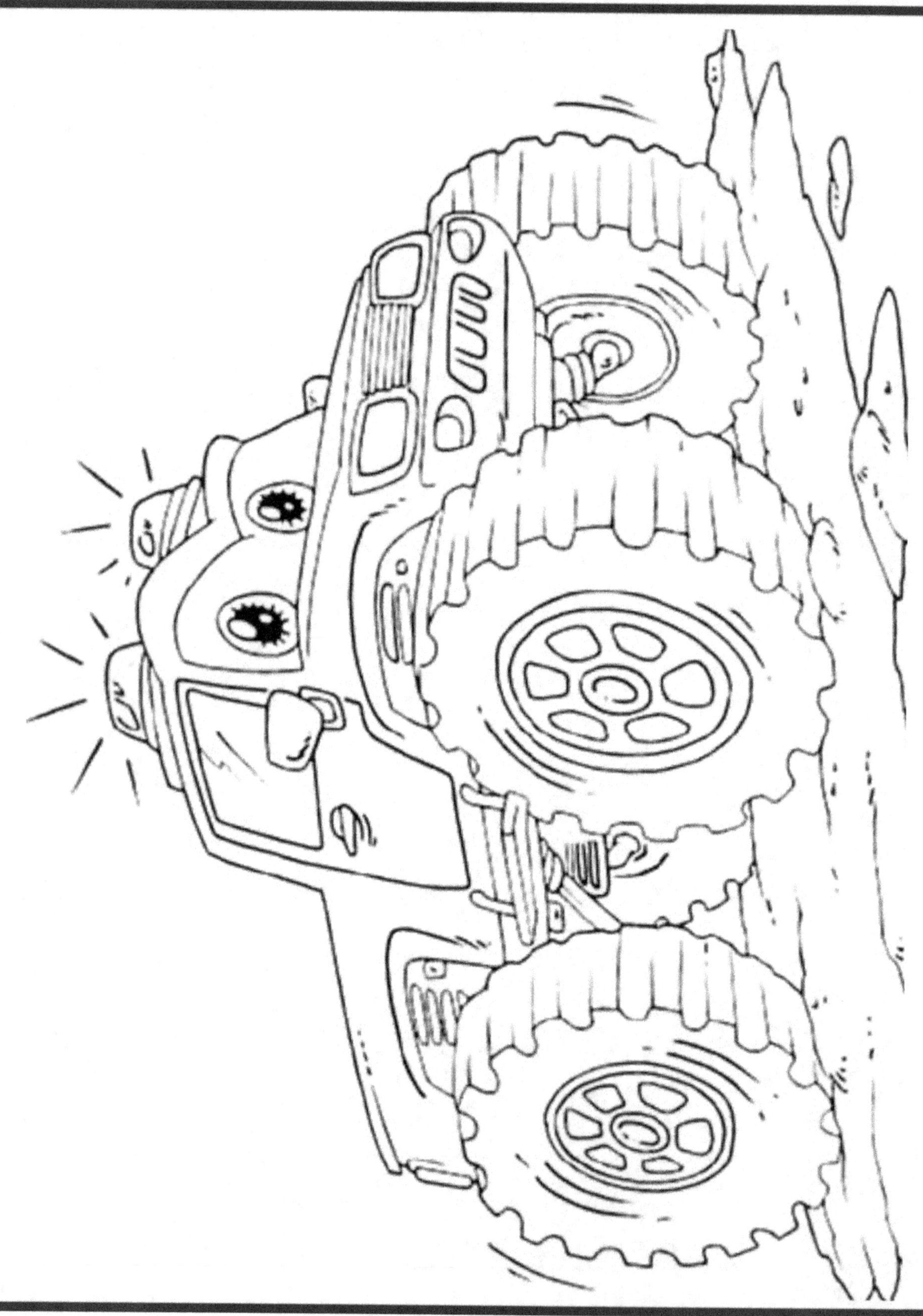

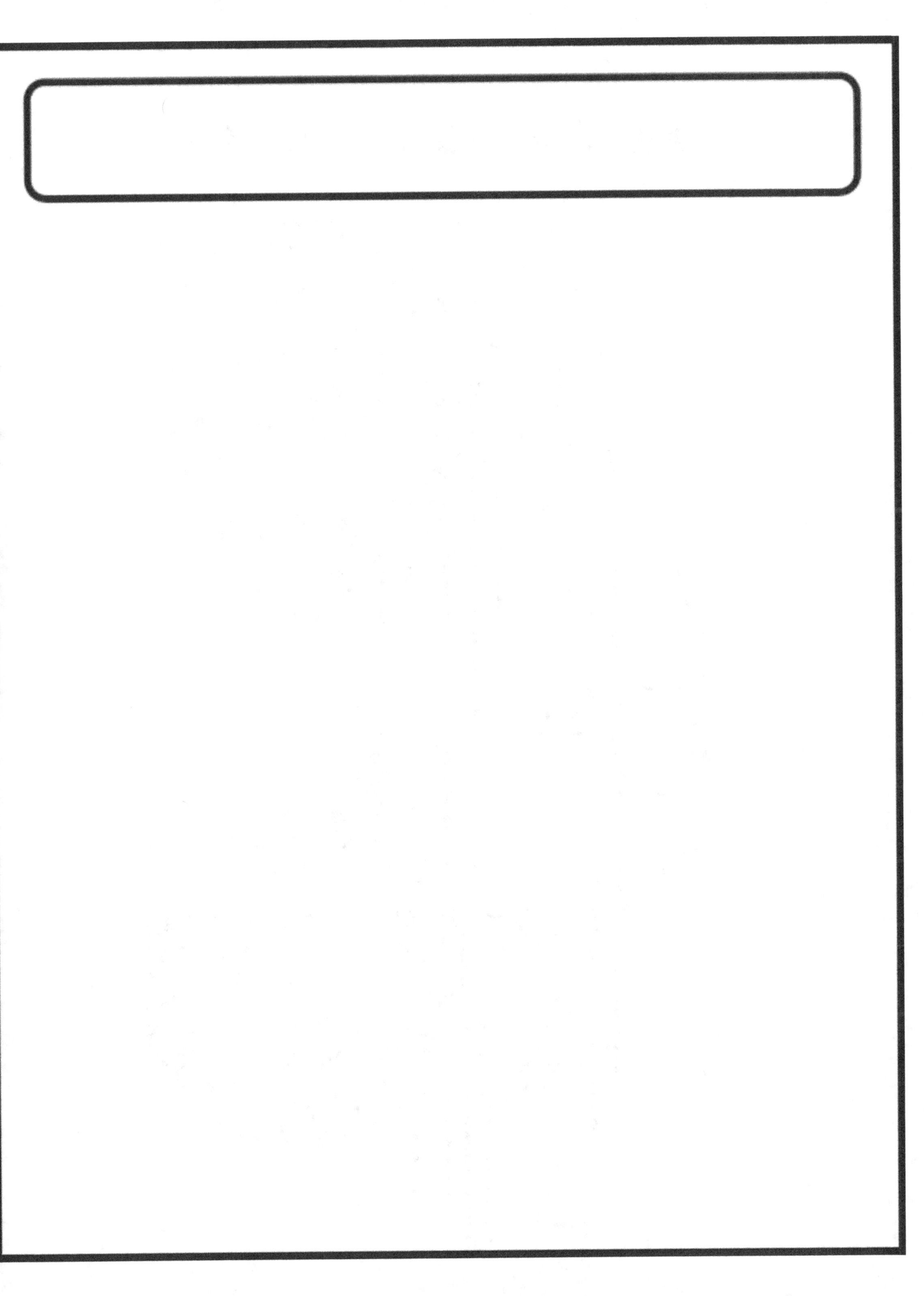

MONSTER TRUCK MALBUCH

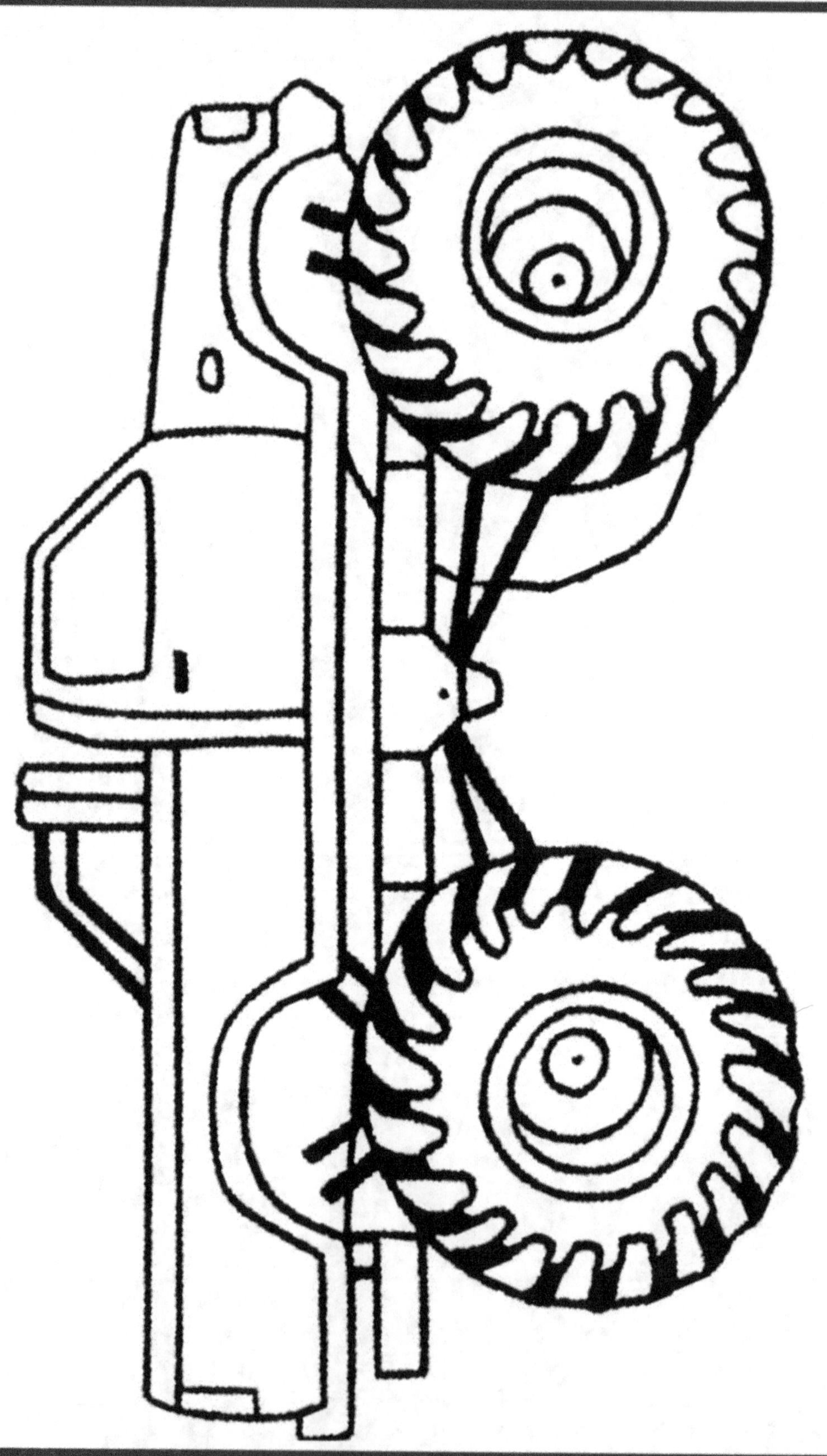

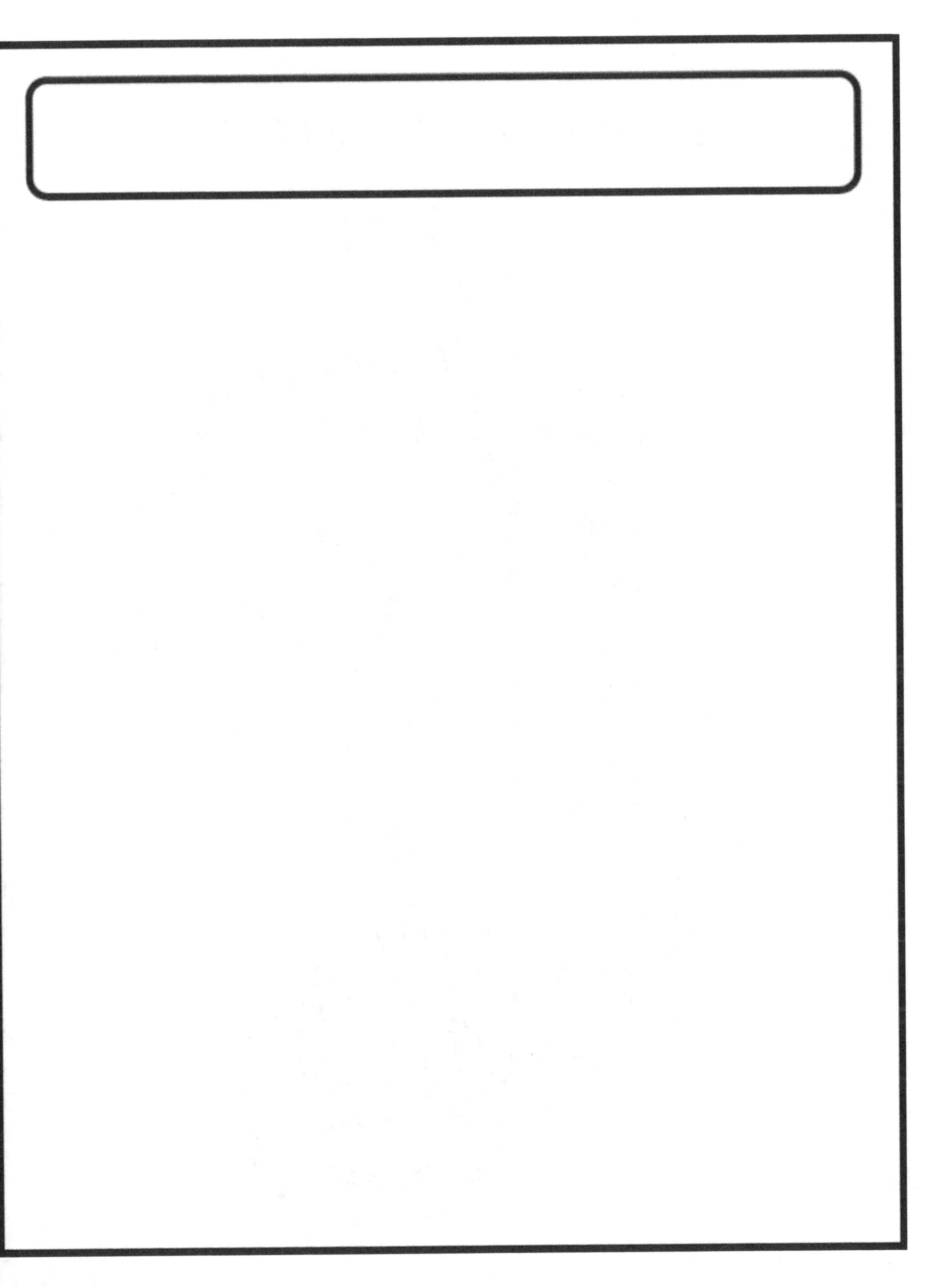

MONSTER TRUCK MALBUCH

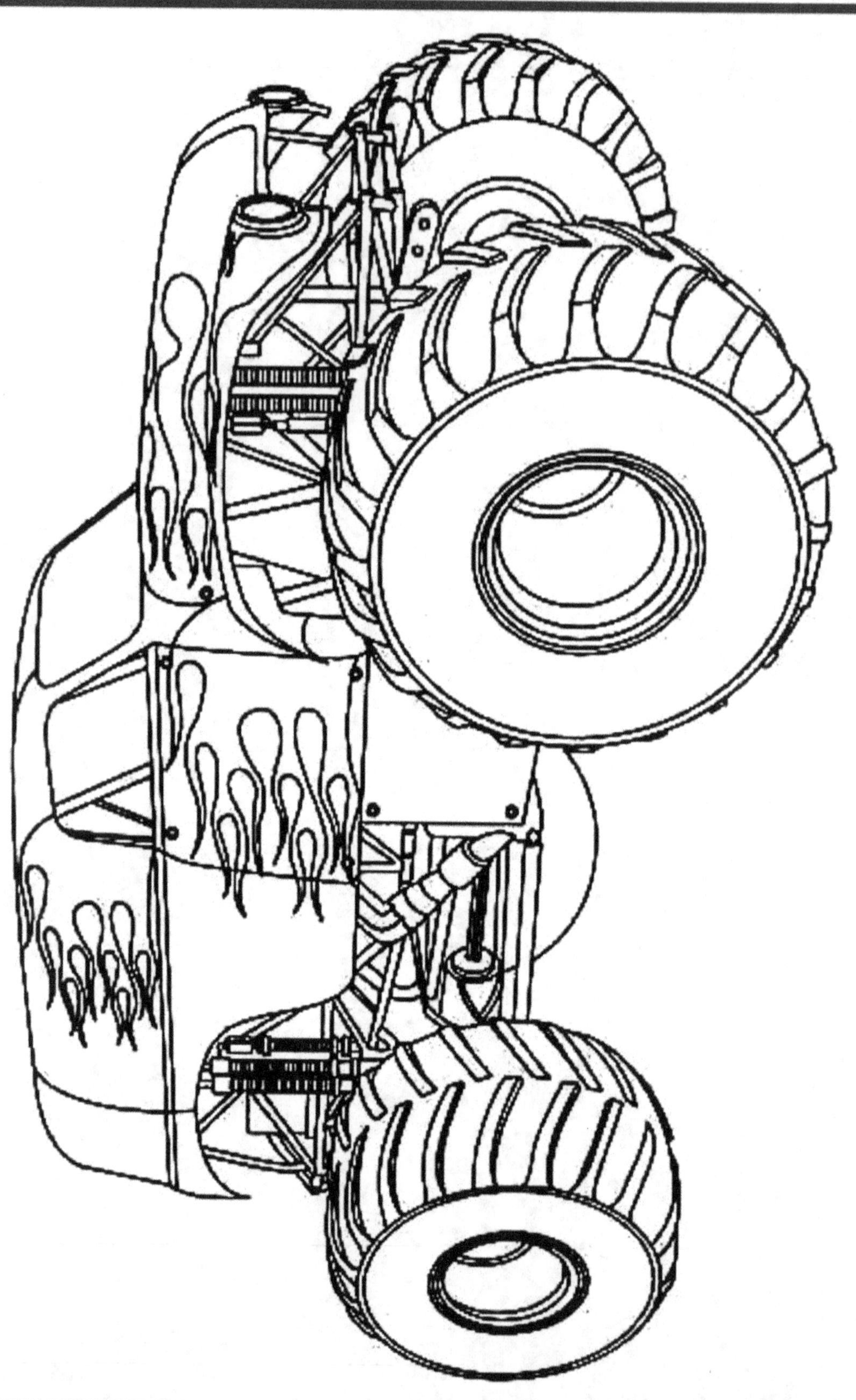

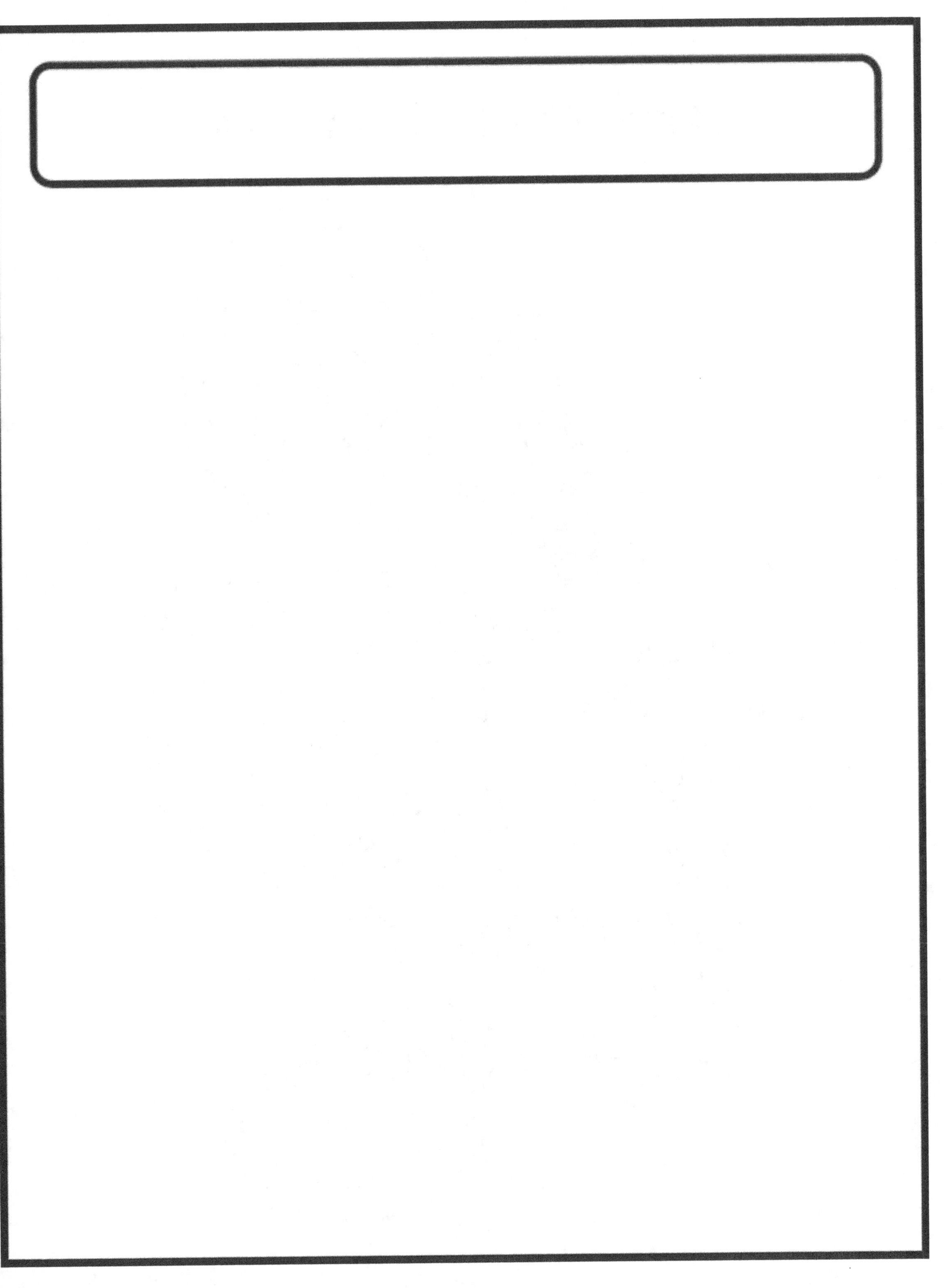

MONSTER TRUCK MALBUCH

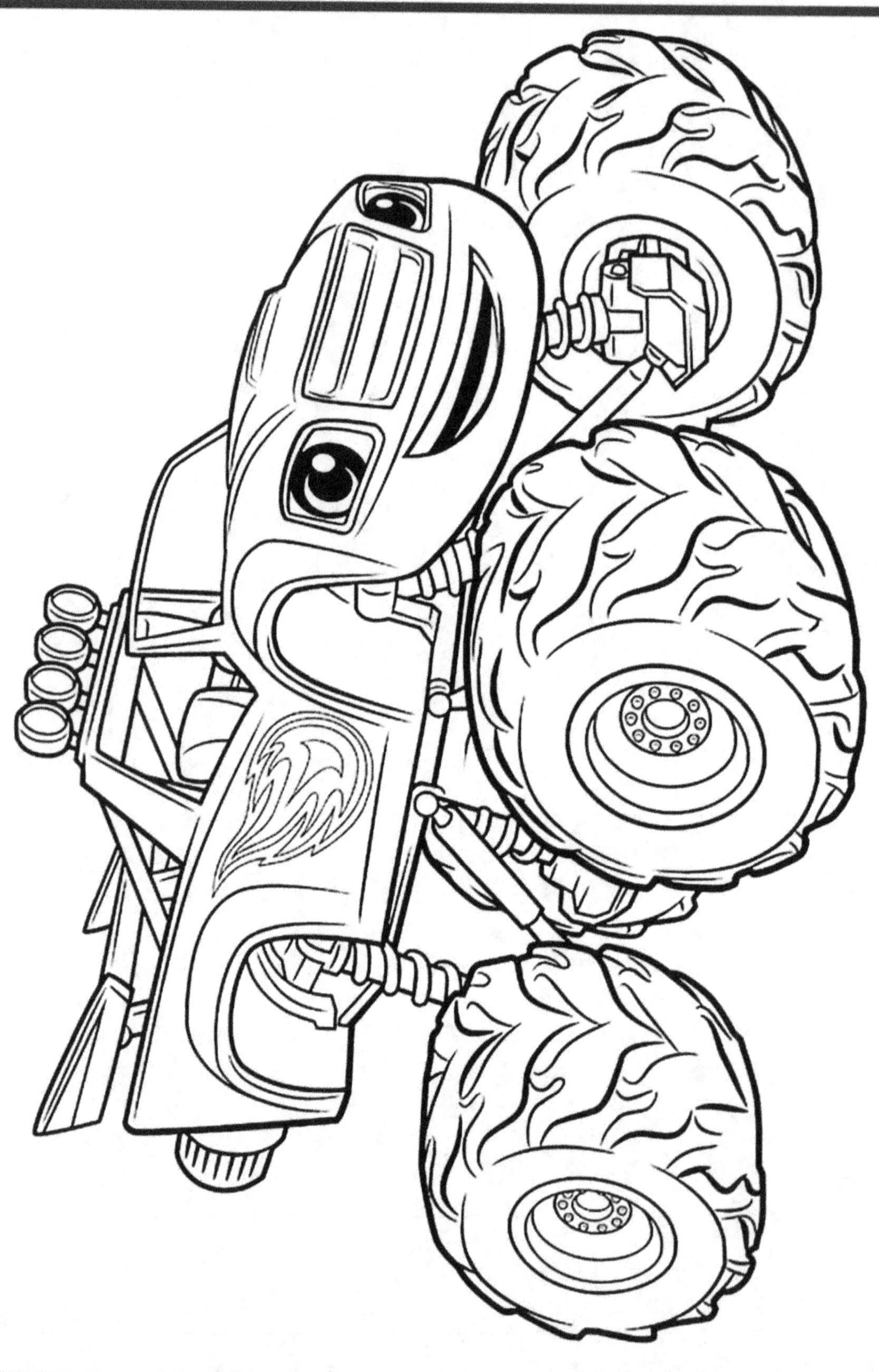

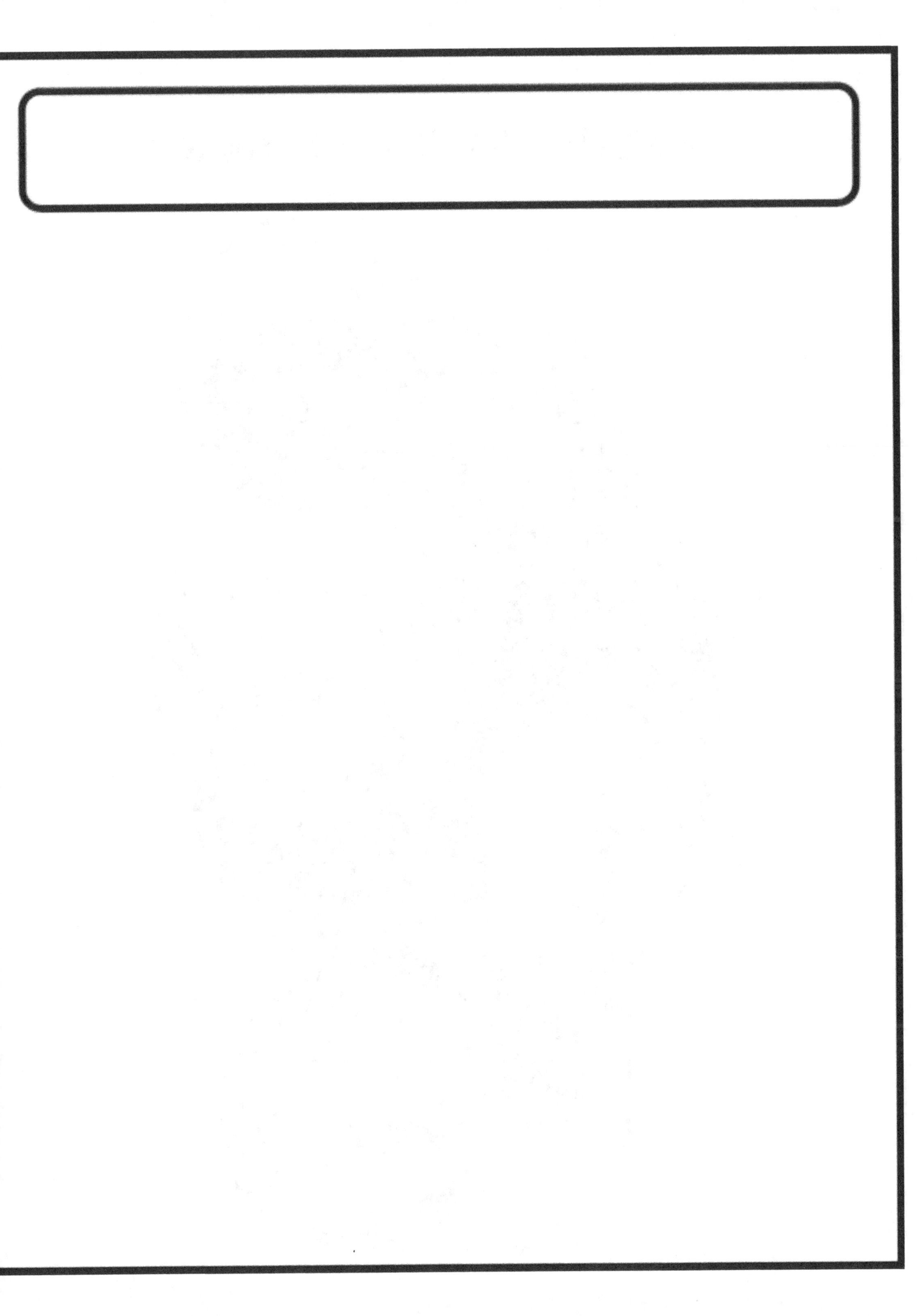

MONSTER TRUCK MALBUCH

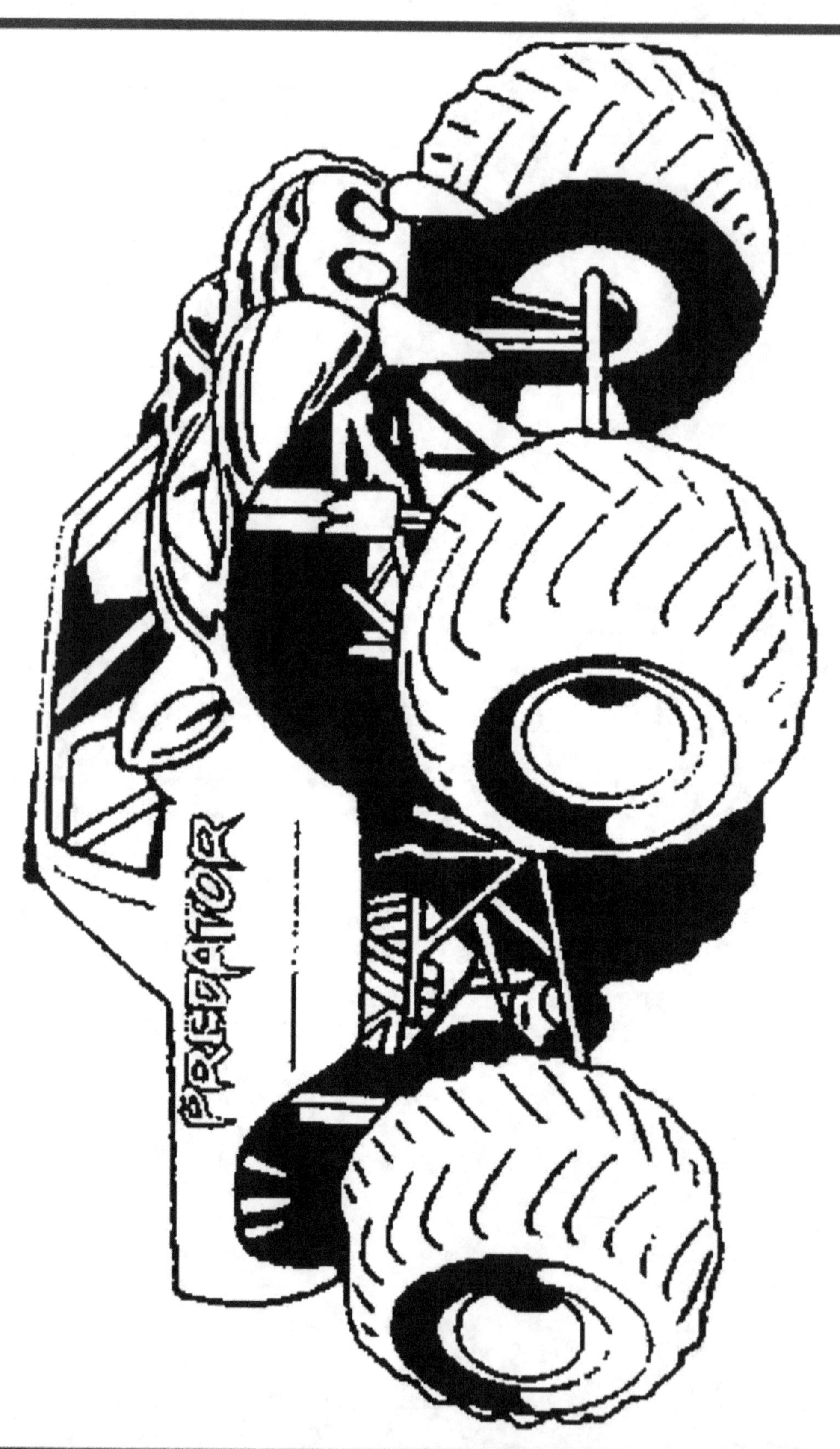

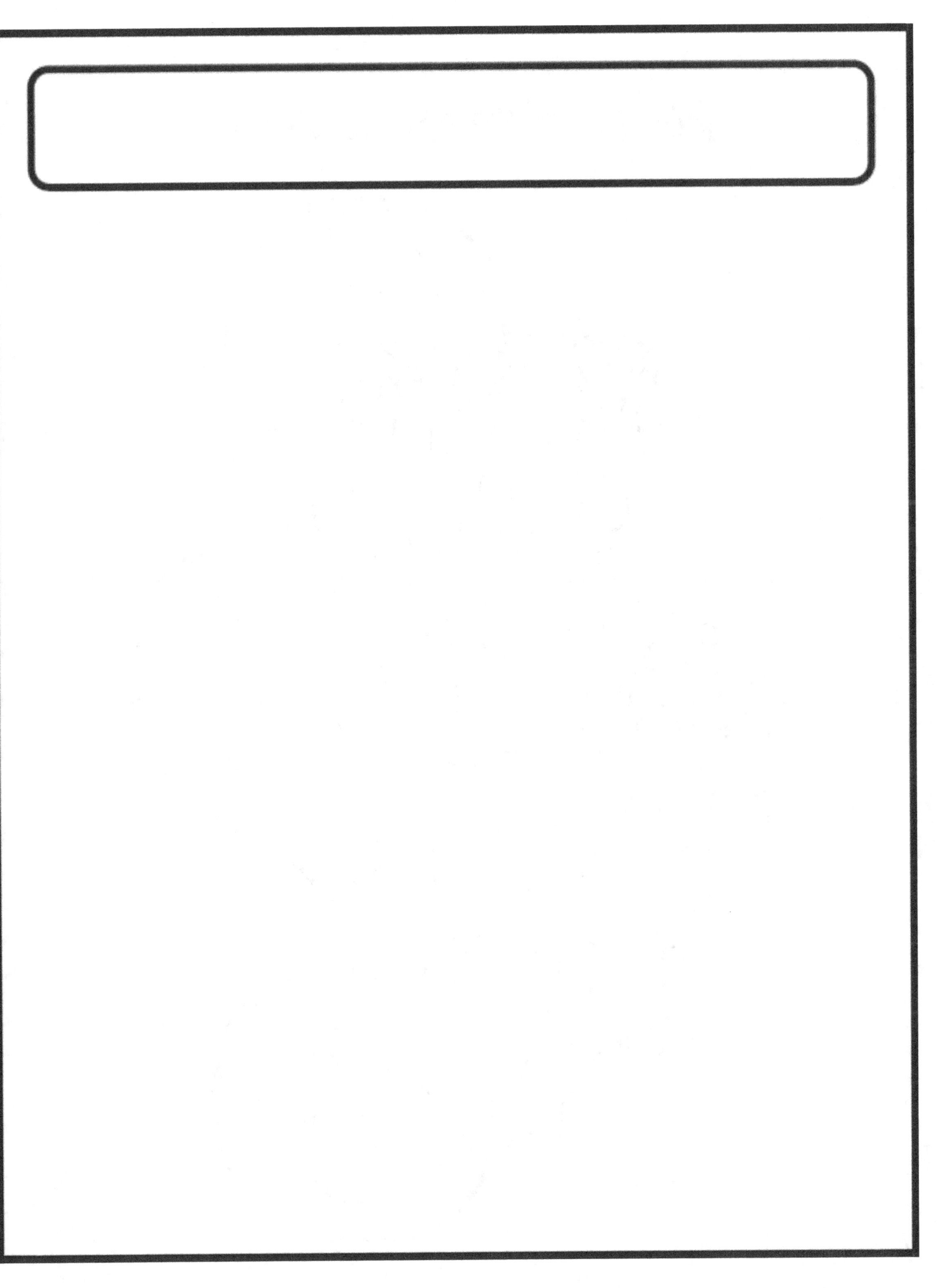

MONSTER TRUCK MALBUCH

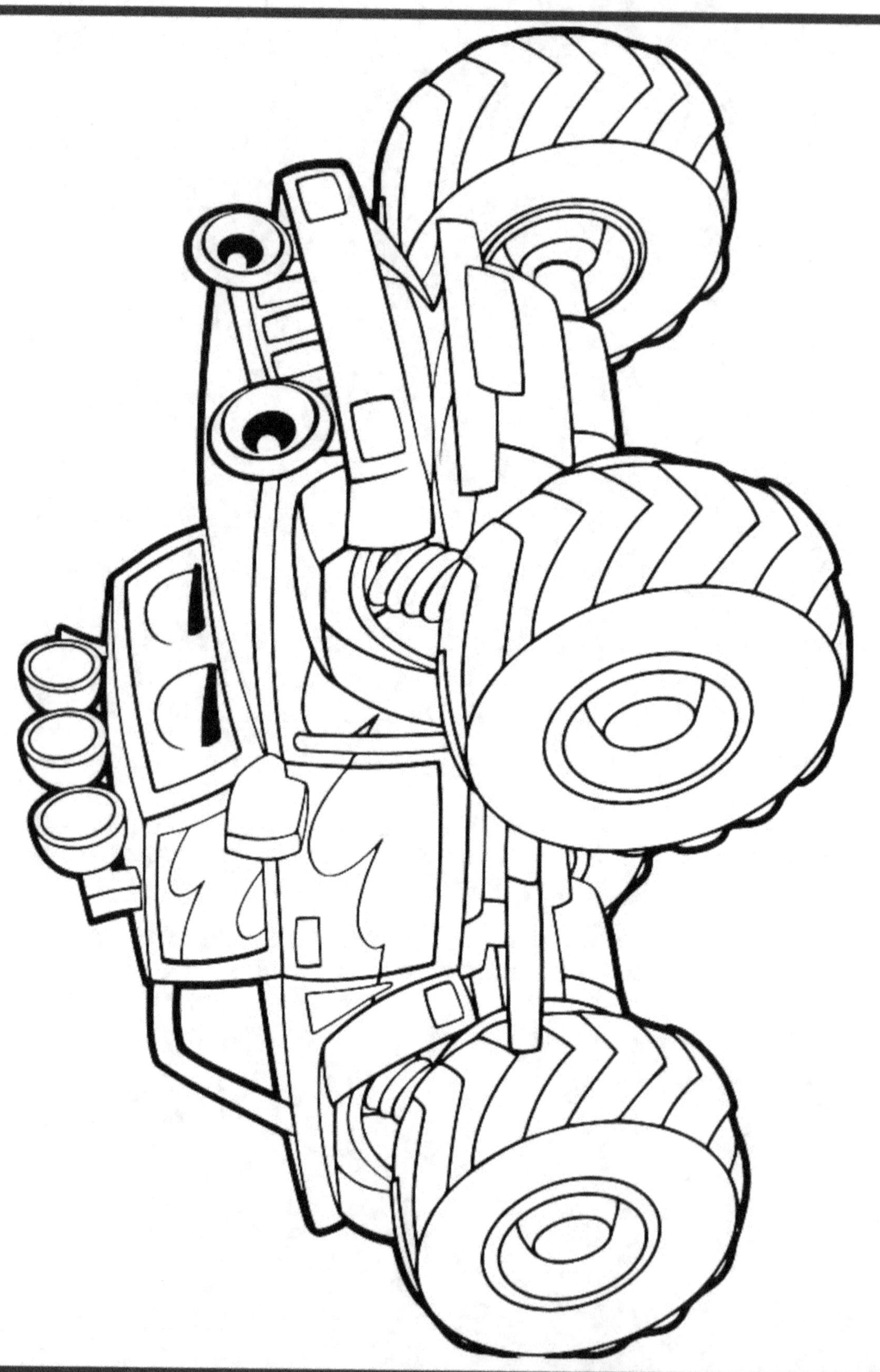

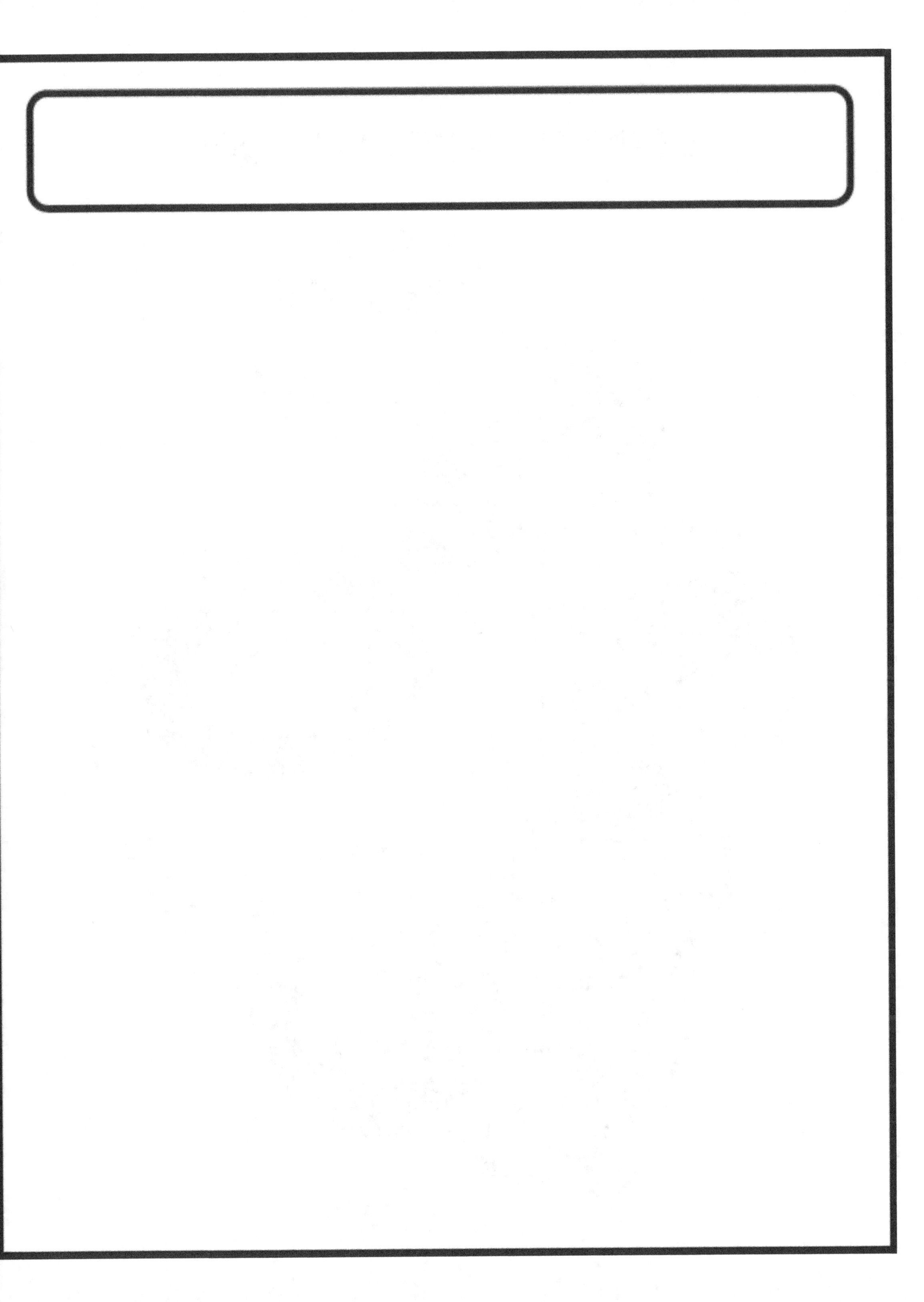

MONSTER TRUCK MALBUCH

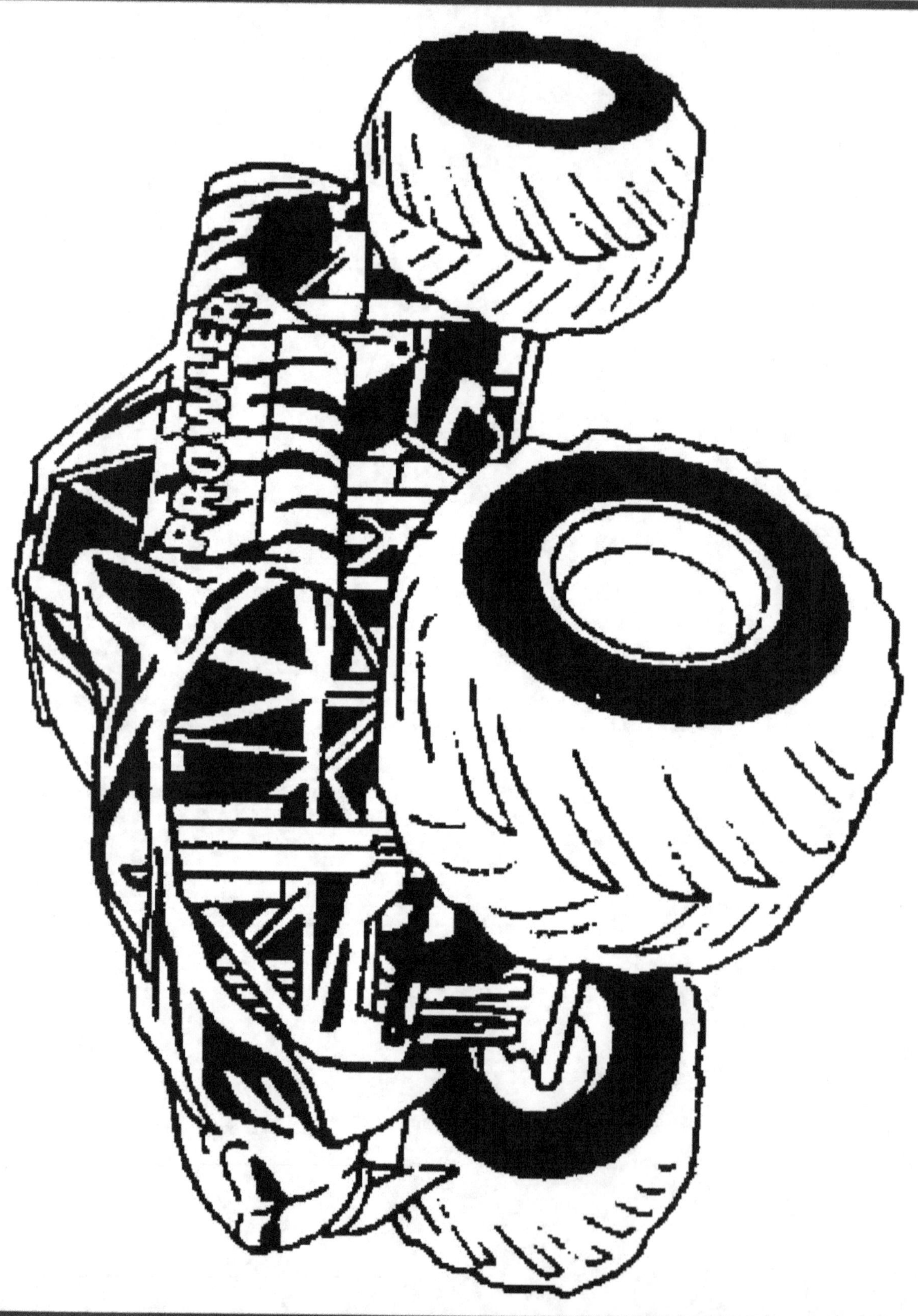

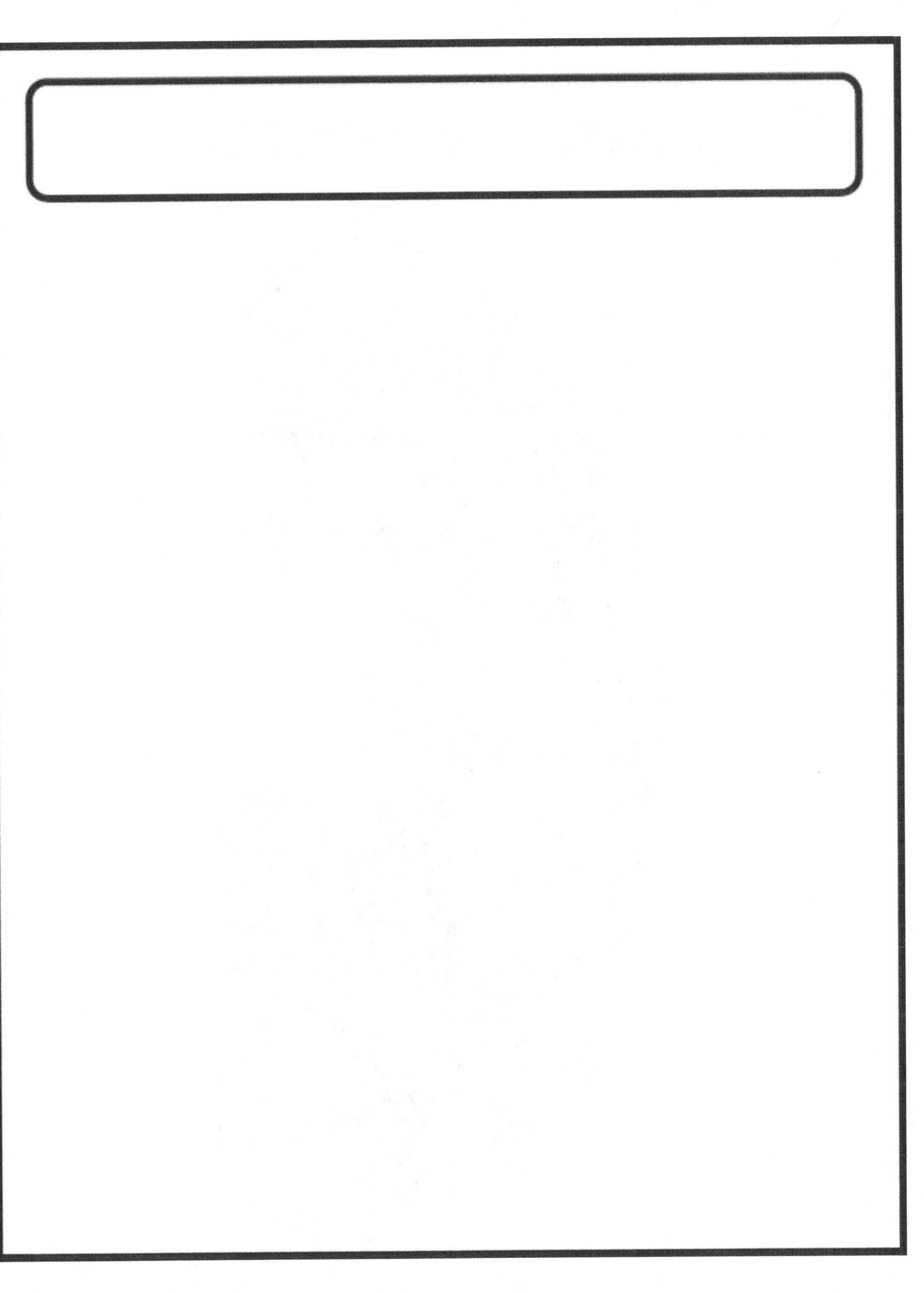

MONSTER TRUCK MALBUCH

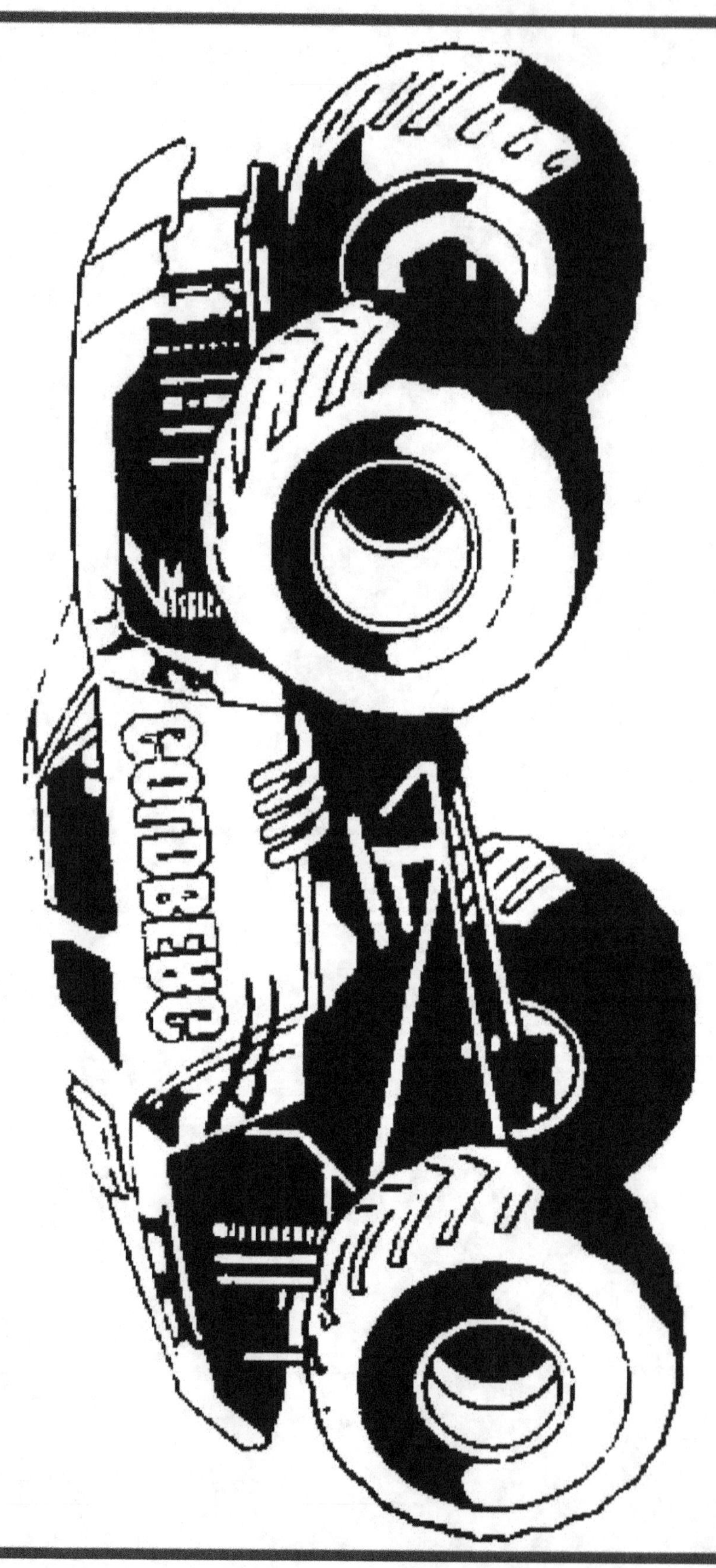

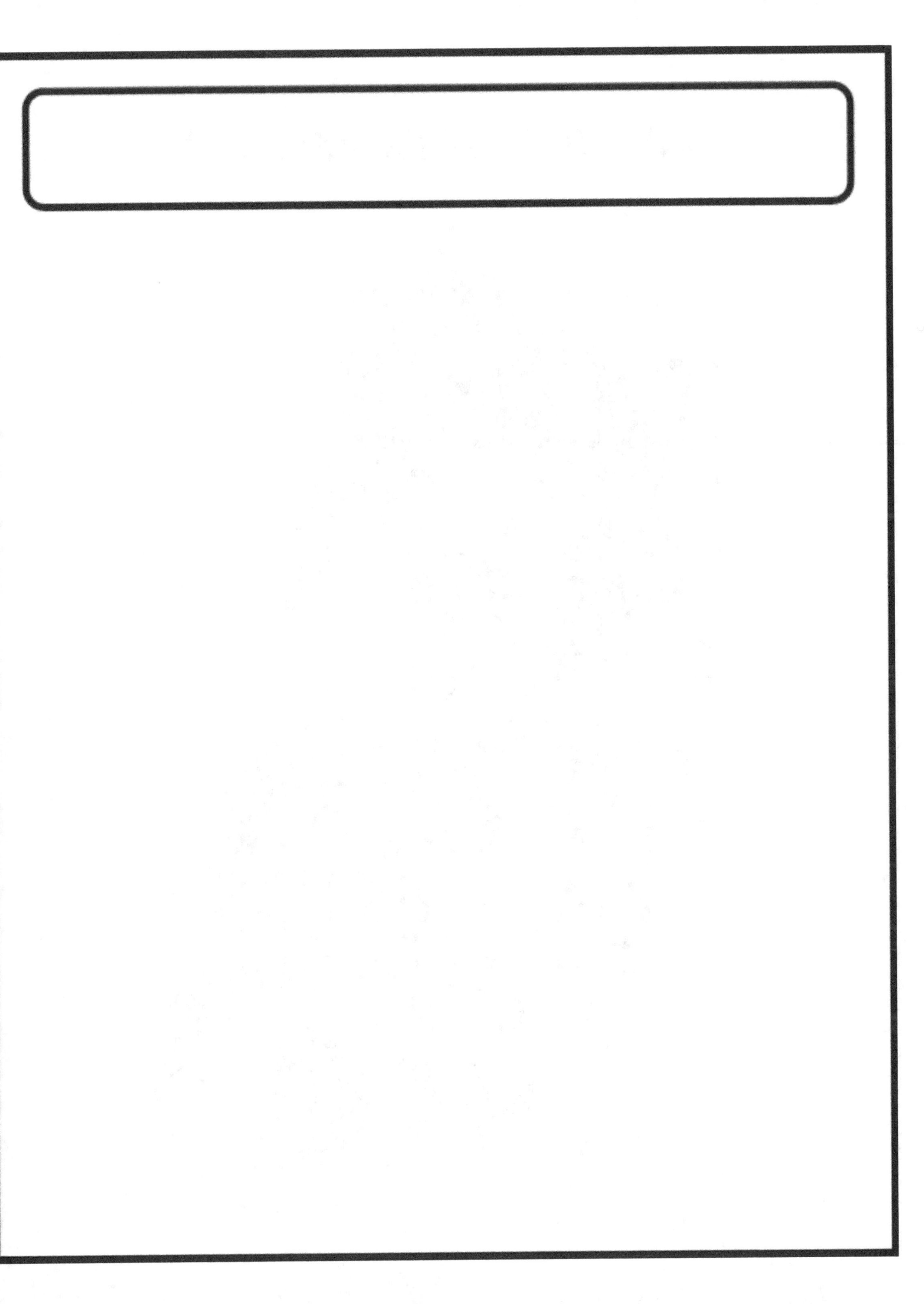

MONSTER TRUCK MALBUCH

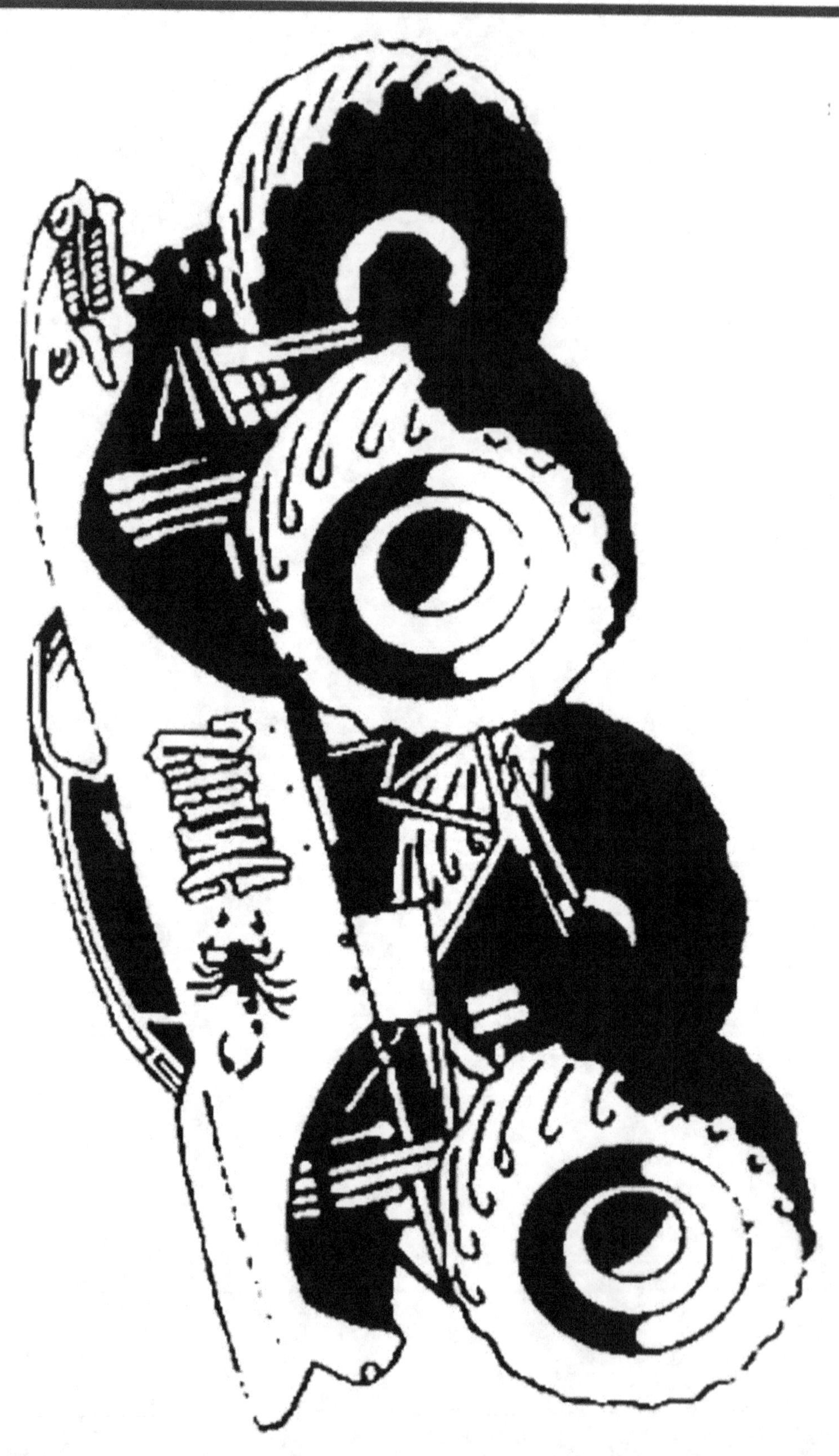

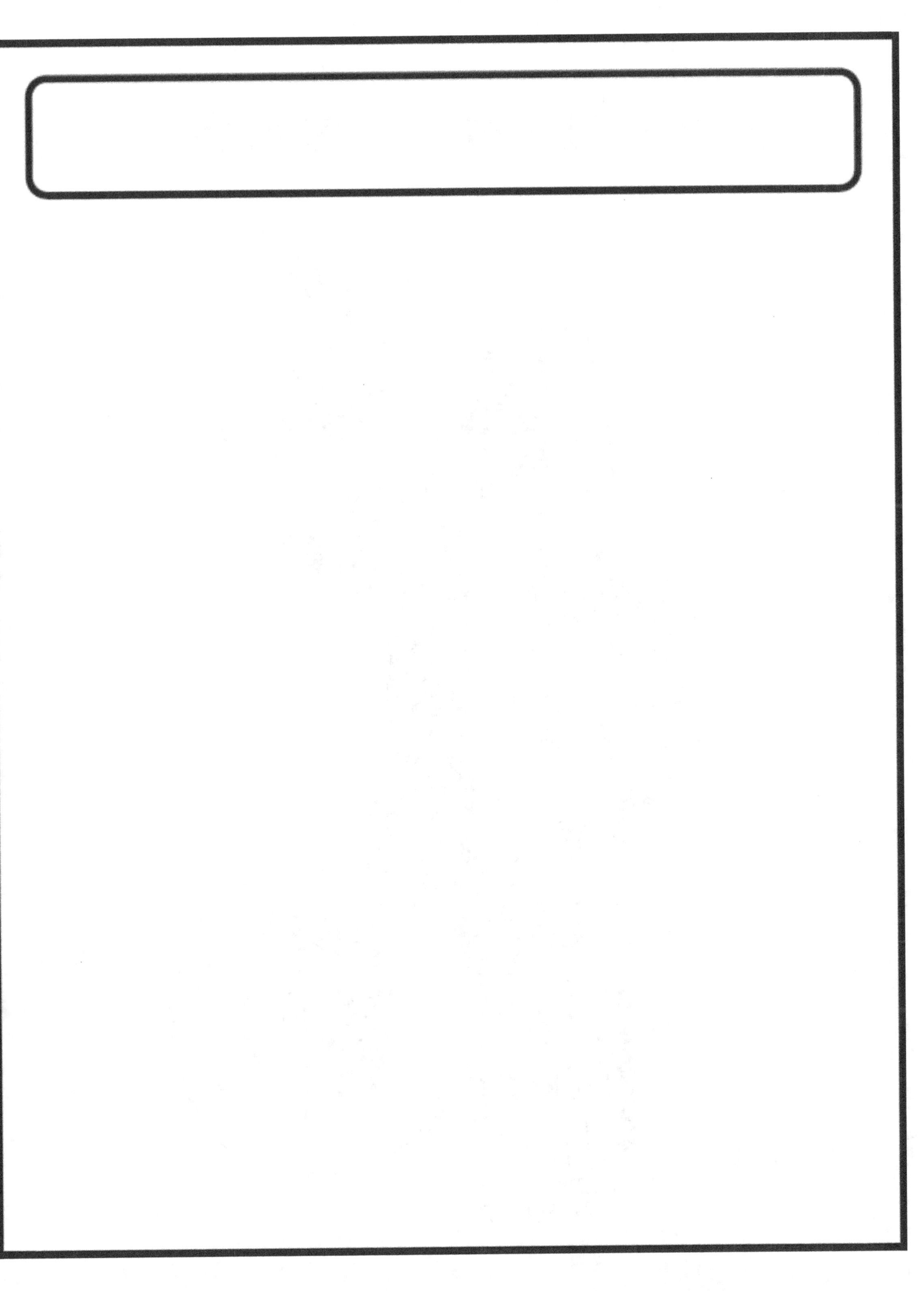

MONSTER TRUCK MALBUCH

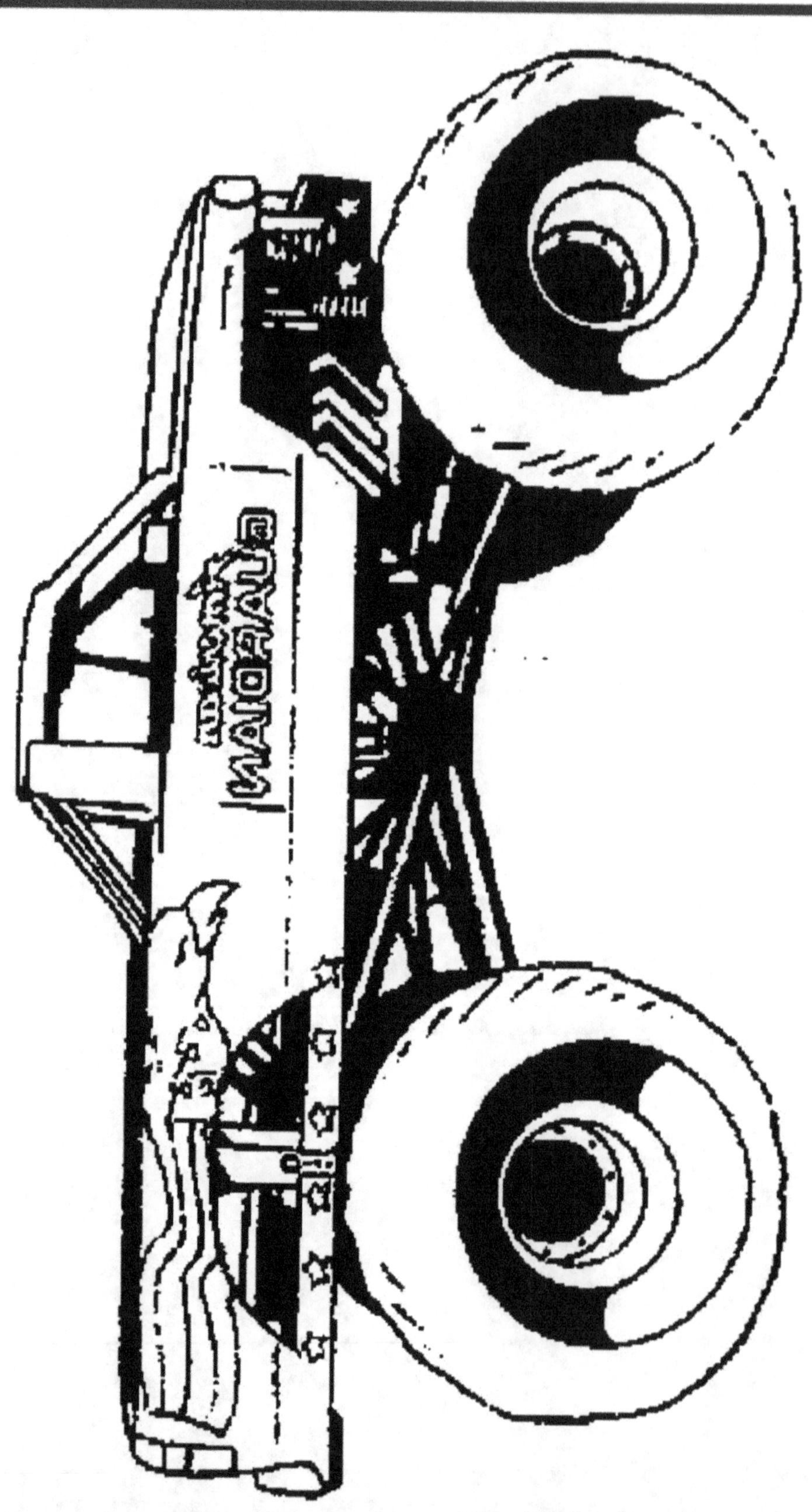

MONSTER TRUCK MALBUCH

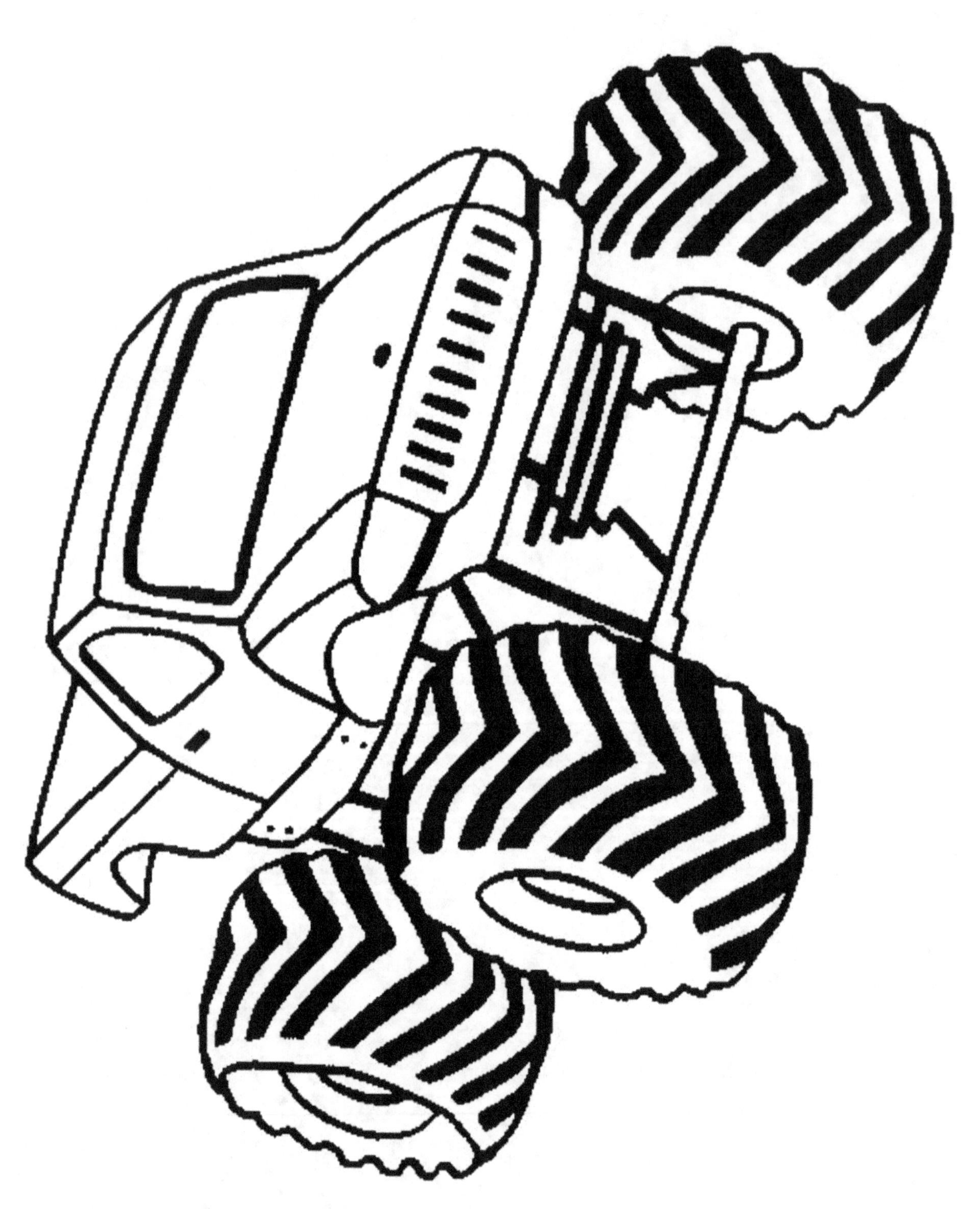

MONSTER TRUCK MALBUCH

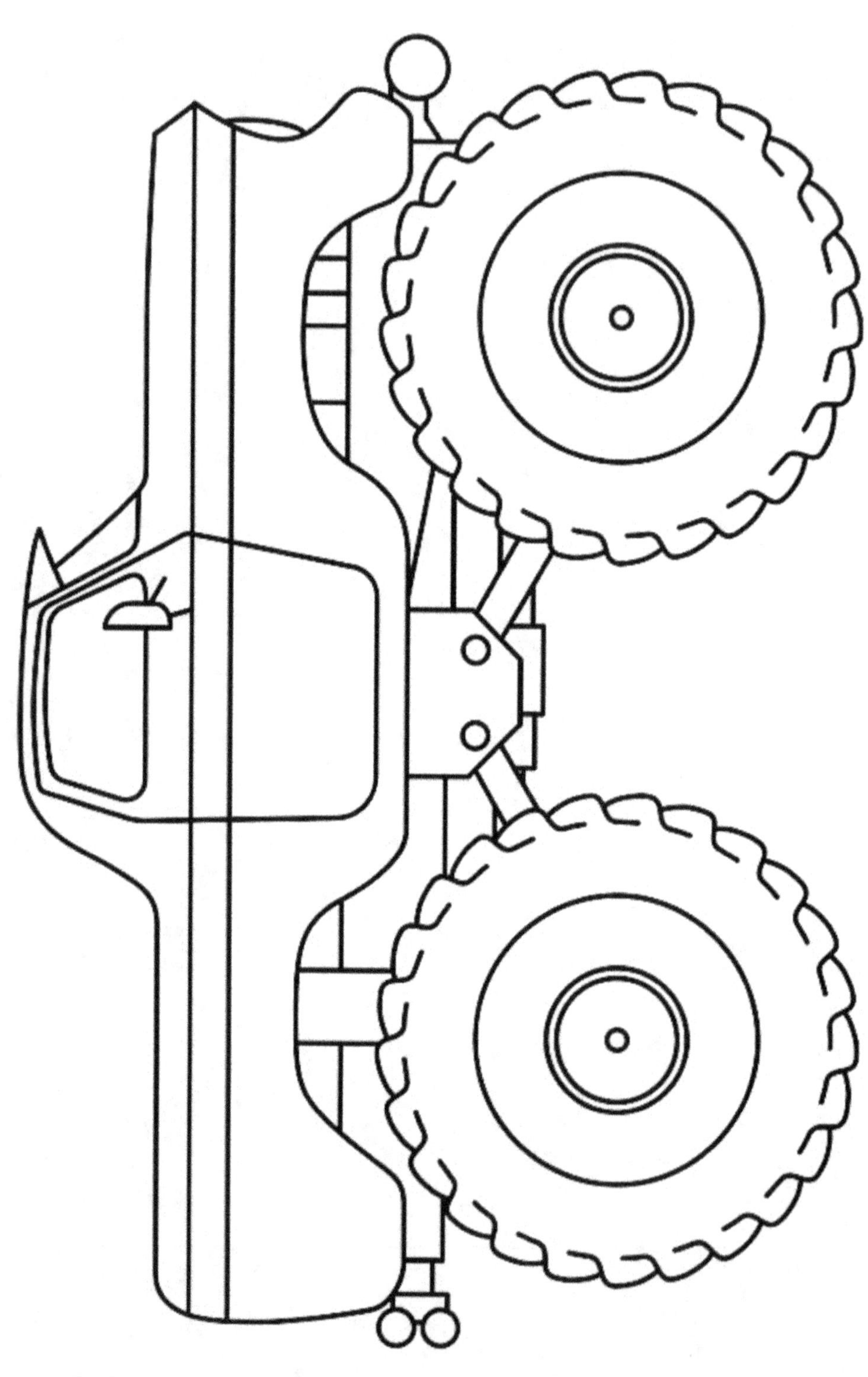

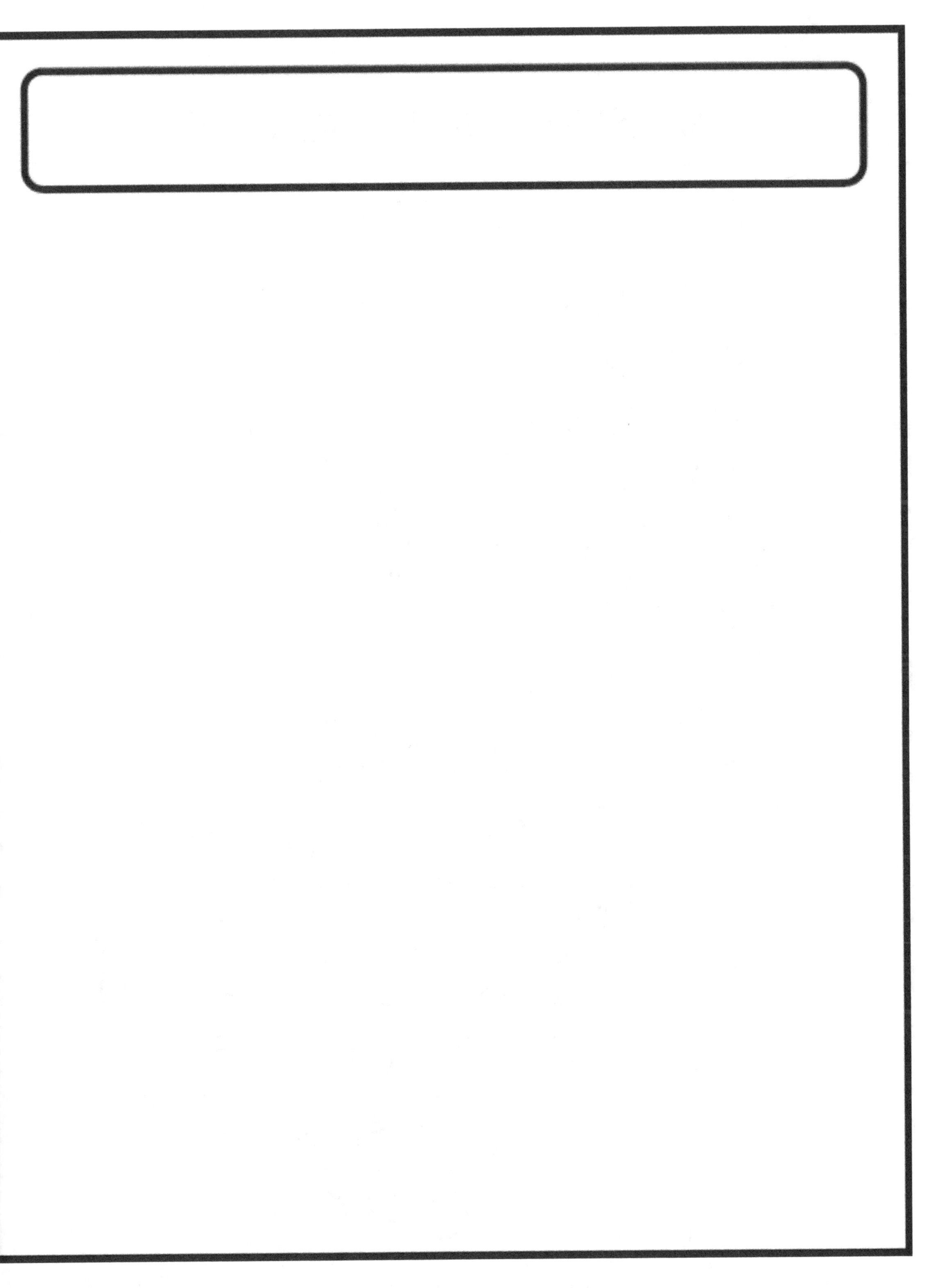

MONSTER TRUCK MALBUCH

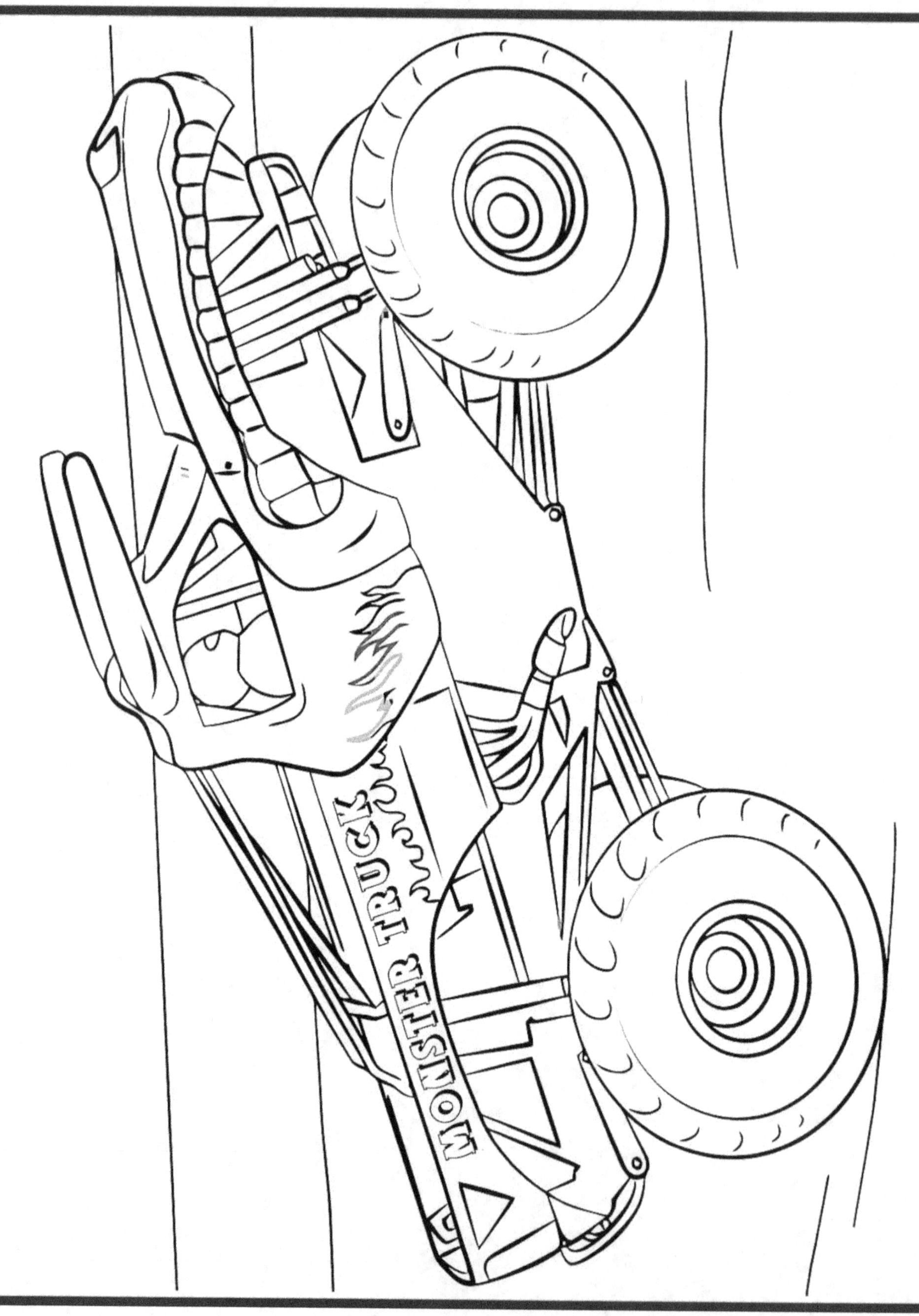

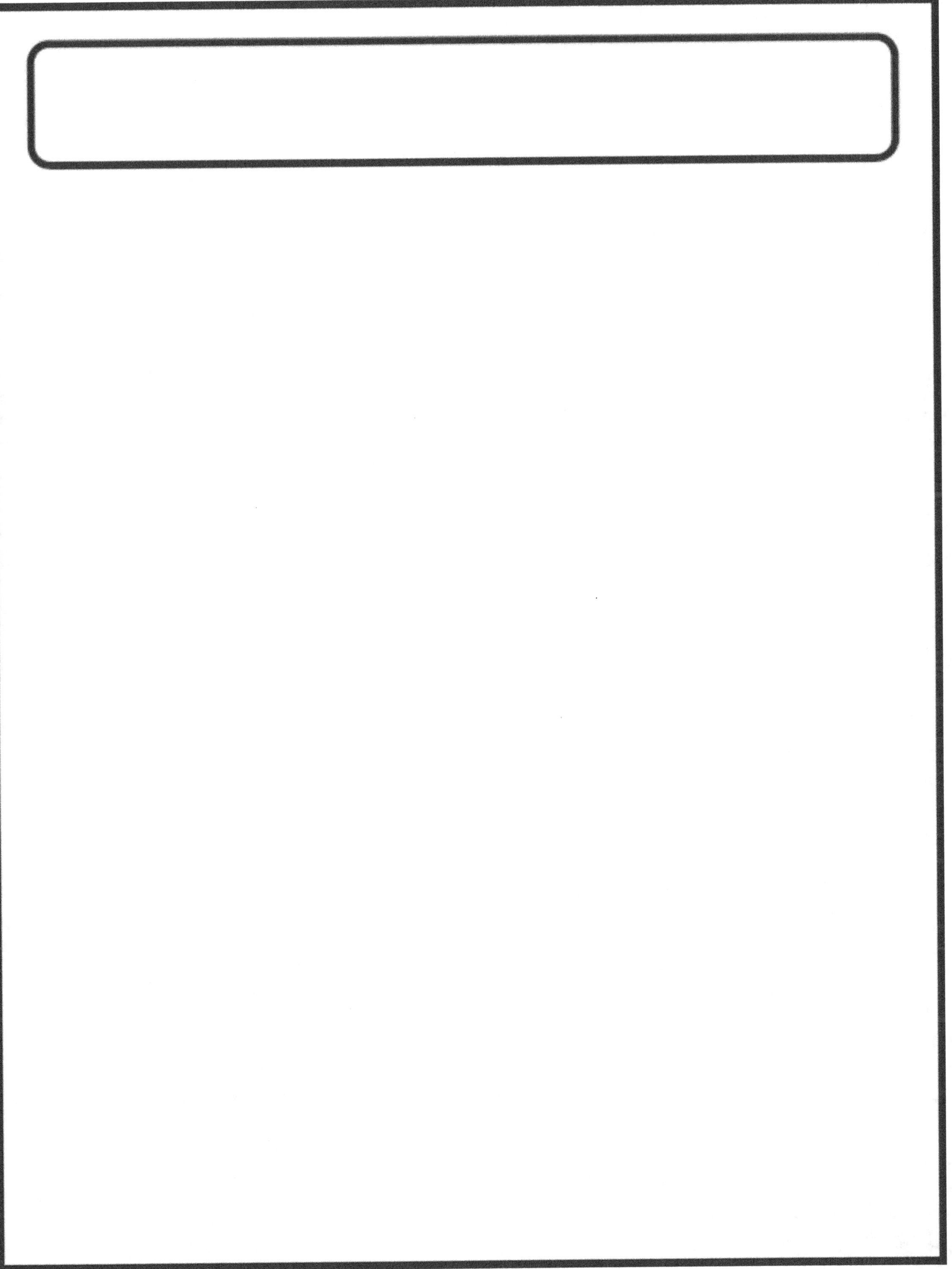